Taki was born in 1937 in Athens. In his earlier years he was a notable sportsman, representing his country in the Davis Cup and, as a skier, in the Winter Olympics; he also had a long spell as captain of the Greek karate team. He has been writing professionally for twenty years, contributing to the American magazines *Esquire*, *Vanity Fair*, *Fame* and *Interview*. His regular column 'High Life' has been running in the *Spectator* since 1977. Taki has homes in New York, London and Gstaad.

HIGH LIFE

TAKI

SELECTED BY ANDREW CAMERON
ILLUSTRATED BY MICHAEL HEATH

PENGUIN BOOKS

For Richard Nixon,
the only President who wrote
to me in prison

PENGUIN BOOKS

Published by the Penguin Group
Penguin Books Ltd, 27 Wrights Lane, London W8 5TZ, England
Viking Penguin, a division of Penguin Books USA Inc.
375 Hudson Street, New York, New York 10014, USA
Penguin Books Australia Ltd, Ringwood, Victoria, Australia
Penguin Books Canada Ltd, 2801 John Street, Markham, Ontario, Canada L3R 1B4
Penguin Books (NZ) Ltd, 182–190 Wairau Road, Auckland 10, New Zealand

Penguin Books Ltd, Registered Offices: Harmondsworth, Middlesex, England

These pieces first appeared in the *Spectator* 1983, 1984, 1985, 1986, 1987, 1988, 1989, 1990
This collection first published by Viking 1989
Published with some additional material in Penguin Books 1990
1 3 5 7 9 10 8 6 4 2

Printed in England by Clays Ltd, St Ives plc

· Contents ·

Contents

· Introduction ·

The 1980s were a period of learning for me, not unlike going back to school for a refresher course on living well. For example: I learned in 1984 that laws are made for everyone, not just for the poor and underprivileged. Now, some of you may think I should have known that for starters – and I agree I should have – but high lifers have a tendency to forget such simple matters.

I think having gone to prison in 1984 for drug possession changed my outlook on life as much as anything has. Previous to that, I had always tried to live on the edge, taking as many chances as possible, and somehow thinking I was above it all where things like luck were concerned.

Gambling had taken me to the brink many times, but on every occasion I had managed to extricate myself on the very last throw of the dice. But on 23 July 1984, I crapped out. When an eagle-eyed Customs officer pointed out to me that an envelope sticking out of my rear pocket was about to fall out, I couldn't help but do a Taki and say, 'Oh, thank you – if only you knew what was in it.' The officer crooked his finger. 'Come back here,' he said. And that was it. My belated education had begun.

Many friends, including some journalists who should know better, insisted I got a raw deal and was made a scapegoat. Not being a professional criminal, I should not go to the slammer because there was nothing to be learned from it, they said. (A fine and some community service, perhaps.) I say, 'Horse feathers!' because 'horse shit' is too strong a term for a high-life book. Had I not been sent to prison I most likely would have broken the law again, and immediately. I found prison so horrible I decided no drug was worth crossing a border with. (Or even taking, for that matter, although I must admit I have sinned since, but very rarely.)

As it turned out, I started a trend. Society being basically made up of copycats, in no time at all peers and socialites were following me to jail for drug offences.

By the autumn of 1985 my education was broadening. I was learning about marriage and something called discretion. Until then

NORMA...

MAILER

CLUNK!

PRINCESS MARGARET

ANNABEL'S

JOHN ASPINALL

GIANNI AGNELLI

RICHARD NIXON

Introduction

I had always felt free not only to have mistresses and girlfriends while happily married, but to write about it, too. My long-suffering wife who, before becoming Mrs Taki, had the rather grand title of Her Serene Highness Princess Alexandra Schoenburg-Hartenstein, finally had enough and sued me for divorce, something neither myself nor my father could understand. After all, I loved Alexandra and provided for her in the style she was accustomed to, so why all the fuss?

Well, I guess even Austrian princesses can be corrupted by American feminists, and Alexandra has been living in New York since the birth of our second child in 1980. So I had to do a *mea culpa*, promise to behave myself, and learn a horrible habit, discretion. As in every other crisis of my life, this one, too, had a happy ending. Alexandra saw the light and preferred to stay with the devil she knew.

Two years later, I studied and became an expert of the human body, or rather, the heart. I had been overdoing things, as always, drinking a lot and late into the night, getting up to train in Karate every morning. It was in Athens, the most polluted city of Western Europe, as well as the hottest. One day, my daddy came to visit me, took one look and ordered me on his boat for a badly needed rest, away from the high life. (Some high life in the Big Olive.)

Swimming off the island of Spetsai, I had a heart attack – rather boringly described in the text – and from that moment on things simply have not been the same. In some way they are better. Mortality causes one to appreciate parties and girls more, and ever since my swim off Spetsai I have been more eclectic in what I drink and who I fall in love with.

On the down side, I now stay in bed for one whole day after a hard night's work, and do not train in the gym or on the tennis court without having slept.

Not that I mind missing the little action there is nowadays, especially in the Big Bagel. Once upon a time, New York was a great place to have fun in, but no longer. Café society – as that amalgam of high and low lifers who regularly entertained and went out nightly was called – has gone the way of democratic Cuban leaders. The Big Bagel's evening hours are now taken up purely with the charity ball, which in most cases is hardly charitable except to the social ambitions of *nouveau riche* Wall Street insider traders.

The nightclub scene, too, has suffered. It is mostly gay and black, and as I am neither, I stay at home a lot and think nostalgically back to the nights when one could drift down to El Morocco or Studio 54 and run into some friends.

Well, perhaps it's all for the better. Annabel's is still going strong: Harry Worcester still at time ululates in the outside bar – although less and less as he is now a married man and a father, to boot – and John, Nando, Ted, and the rest of the impeccable Birley team still humour the old crowd that complains the place is now full of stock-brokers. Tramps is back in style because the young inherit a night-club, and I now frequent it because all my friends' sons and daughters do. The only thing that scares me is the fact that soon they, too, will marry and have children, and it just might look too ridiculous for words for me to be seen going out with *their* offspring. But then, perhaps not.

1983

· Star player ·

New York · Porfirio Rubirosa, the much married Dominican polo player, was probably the greatest playboy of all time. He was also a modern Robin Hood. He took from the very, very rich, and gave to the not nearly as rich – namely himself. Rubi, as all his close friends called him, was best man when I married my first wife. Recently I have been having nostalgic reminiscences about him. I just finished reading a book entitled *Poor Little Rich Girl*, a biography of Barbara Hutton, Rubirosa's fourth wife, as well as one of the richest women on earth.

Thinking back, I thank my lucky stars that Rubi liked staying out even later than I did – because if he hadn't, I probably wouldn't be around now to tell you about him. Let me explain. It was in the early hours of 6 July 1965. Rubi and I were celebrating in New Jimmy's, the best nightclub of the period, in Boulevard Montparnasse. The day before, our team had won the Open Polo Championship of Paris. Our wives had gone home around four in the morning, but Rubi wanted to go on. I remember it as if it were yesterday. I had to fly to Nice that day and compete in a tennis tournament. My aeroplane was due to leave at 8 a.m., and as I was staying with Rubi in his house at St Cloud, I would just about make it. At six, I insisted I had to leave. His last words to me were, 'What a selfish shit you are.' I caught a taxi back and went on to Nice eventually. Rubi left an hour after me, and as was his custom, drove at high speed through the Bois de Boulogne to St Cloud. While passing the Bagatelle Polo Club he hit a tree head on. He died on the way to hospital. When I saw the wreck I realized that no one could have survived it – especially as my side was more badly smashed than his.

Although I was overcome with grief, I did not regret leaving him. Rubi never allowed me to drive when we used to return home together, and he relished performing 'four-wheel drifts' while going round corners in the Bois. There was no way I would have been driving back that night. The *Figaro* wrote that had Rubi been wearing a seat belt he might have survived. It also said that had Rubi been wearing a seat belt he would not have been Rubi.

The newspaper was right. Among Rubi's many charms was a recklessness where danger was concerned, an insouciance toward physical injury and death. I wish I could say the same about today's playboys. He was the quintessential man's man, someone who was adored by men, obviously in a platonic way, almost as much as he was pursued and worshipped by women. He was the most charming man I ever met, a very good polo player and racing driver, the only man I never saw fail with a woman.

His funeral was attended by about 250 people, a small number for a famous playboy. What was extraordinary, however, was the fact that the service was meant to be attended by only the closest of his friends, and the people who showed up all felt that they were. Among them were people like the Maharaja of Jaipur, an old polo buddy of Rubi's, a sprinkling of Kennedys, plus every waiter from *rive gauche* nightclubs that Rubi had befriended late at night. French waiters being what they are, as well as maharajas, it is clear that Rubi was no ordinary chap.

Which brings me to what my friend Gianni Agnelli said recently about those good old days: 'People had fun because they wanted to, while present-day playboys play for the public. Values today are of very bad quality. One may have had bad habits in the old days, but never bad quality.' Gianni should know. If anyone was braver and more reckless in the face of danger than Rubi it was Fiat's chairman. He also was a great playboy except for one great fault: work. No sooner would dawn come than Gianni would climb on board his plane and fly back to Turin and be at his desk by 8.30.

Although posterity will hardly remember Rubi as a person who lived a useful life, I, among many others, certainly will. After all, he lived his life the way he saw fit, lived it to the full; was never hypocritical the way so many people are today where money and doing something with it are concerned. And his timing, or exit rather, was perfect. I simply could never see Rubi doing an exhibitionistic, narcissistic solo on a crowded disco floor, or bending over some filthy loò to ingest a white powder – something which every playboy seems to have done ever since 6 July 1965.

1984

· Fun and games ·

As everyone who loves Italian food knows, the Mafia frequent restaurants where the food tends to be perfect and the staff unusually polite. I became aware of this when I was fresh out of Eton and newly arrived in New York. An Argentinian Lothario befriended me and introduced me to his favourite hangout in midtown Manhattan. It served Italian dishes and, more important, was known as the place a lot of models dropped in at for a quick ravioli *à la* Genovese. This was during lunchtime. In the evening the clientele were mostly elderly gentlemen who more often than not did not remove their hats while eating.

That is one thing that sticks in my mind. The other is that whenever the doors swung open and someone came in from outside, people would automatically duck under the tables. After that everyone continued eating and conversing as if nothing had happened. It was a reflex action from men with first-hand knowledge of suppers that had been rudely interrupted by the familiar rat-tat-tat of a sub-machine gun. The women, too, were straight out of Central Casting. The blondes always looked extremely tall while they were seated, but once they stood up one would realize they were of normal height and it was their leonine bouffant *coiffures* that added the inches.

The owner of the place was a Rossano Brazzi lookalike by the name of Armando Orsini. Armando's name was not originally Orsini – as he himself was the first to admit – but upon arriving in a city that had more Italians living within its confines than Rome, he thought it a good idea to give himself a fairer start than he originally had back in Naples. Prince Raimondo Orsini was in the news back then for escorting Soraya, the Shah's recently divorced wife, so Armando picked Orsini more or less for the name's topicality. (Years later, when the real Orsini had made a complete fool of himself by hanging around nightclubs with Soraya-like intellectuals, everyone referred to Armando as the real Orsini, and to Raimondo as the phoney one.)

Armando was extremely good-looking and, like most Italians born without a silver spoon, looked aristocratic because of his masculine

7

and clean-cut looks. His lack of English helped. Those were the days when an Italian accent got one respect rather than snickers. It was also the time when an innocent American public believed that the Mafia were involved in bootlegging and *c'est tout*. As my friend Frank Costello used to say, 'If it was good enough for Joe Kennedy, it's good enough for me.'

Mr C and I used to dine there quite often, mostly after the Friday-night fights at the old Madison Square Garden. The waiters would literally jump whenever the *cappo di tutti cappi* asked for his favourite spinach-and-cheese-filled pasta. There was a bartender called Joe who looked like the spitting image of Ernest Borgnine, the actor, and a head waiter called Ignacio who had been slapped more times than Anthony Haden-Guest's cheques have bounced. Ignacio was not the smartest of fellows, but he was certainly the most naïve. Costello's favourite joke was an old one. Whenever he spotted a celebrity (Bette Davis, Elizabeth Taylor and Zsa Zsa Gabor happen to come to mind) he would write a note and send it to them with Ignacio, after telling him to wait for an answer without saying where the note came from. Inside he would write the following: 'Although a humble head waiter, I would love to show you how good I am in bed. I need an answer right away. Respectfully yours, Ignacio.'

It was at Orsini's where I met Benedetta Barzini, Luigi's daughter. I will never forget it because it was the night of one of my worst humiliations. We dined early and went to the Garden with the Godfather and one of Mr C's henchmen. Benedetta had no idea who they were, and had never before been to the fights. As old hands, Mr C and I carried newspapers underneath our arms in case the fight got too bloody – which, as luck would have it, it did. We were in the first row and as soon as was necessary I unfolded my paper and shielded Signorina Barzini and myself. But to my horror she would have none of my protection. Instead, she climbed up on the ring and ... after yelling to the ref to stop the fight tried to stop it herself. I was so ashamed I tried to hide underneath my seat. Mr C looked as if the fuzz had caught him red-handed. Tough guys' molls simply don't act that way. I should have known better. The henchman looked at me as if I had called the cops – who by that time were climbing on to the ring to bring my date back. I not only became the laughing stock of the Garden, but also of Orsini's.

The reason I am yet again reminiscing is that I ran into Armando the other day, and heard that Benedetta's father hasn't been feeling his best lately. Neither has Armando, but when we thought of the fun we once had he brightened up and told me that Ignacio recently figured out why all those film stars used to slap him. 'Mr Costello must have written something rude and they were afraid to answer back,' is what Ignacio finally worked out, according to the real Orsini.

· Fohnies ·

Gstaad · All is quiet in Gstaad. Now that the 'smart' people have left, it is once again possible to find a place in the sun on the terrace of the Arc-en-Ciel for lunch, and a table at the Olden for dinner. The villagers, as always, look happy. They have worked hard throughout the winter months and now that the invaders have left their loot behind and become scarce, it is time to enjoy themselves. This was probably the best season Gstaad has ever had. The up-turn in the American economy, coupled with a snowfall compared only with the one that hit Russia in 1812, helped make this a winter to remember.

Last week, Miss Diana Ross and Mr David Bowie came to Gstaad, and for some strange reason I was invited to a party in their honour. Now there are few things that strike me as more ridiculous than the thought of Diana Ross (a black singer) and David Bowie (a pop star who could be either sex) frolicking in the snows of the Bernese Oberland. To my surprise, however, both turned out to be almost human, extremely polite, and by far the nicest celebrities this Mecca of the rich has seen in a long time. The fact that they came *après saison* should have warned me that they weren't here in order to excite the paparazzi. Miss Ross came with her three children, and Monsieur Bowie with a lady I suppose was his wife.

What struck me about the duo was that neither drove up in the *de rigueur* Rolls – or haemorrhoid, as we call them here because every arsehole sooner or later is bound to get one – nor were they surrounded by the only cultural influence the oily Arabs have bequeathed to the Western world, the bevy of beefy bodyguards.

Like violence that breeds more violence, bodyguards in public places provoke more than they protect. Movie and rock stars use them to carry their drugs across borders, or to pick up girls – or men for that matter – when in nightclubs. The bodyguards are more often than not cowards, people who have failed as athletes or policemen, thus they already carry a chip on their shoulder the size of the mountain I've just skied down from. They look for the best-looking person who might invade what they think is their master's territory

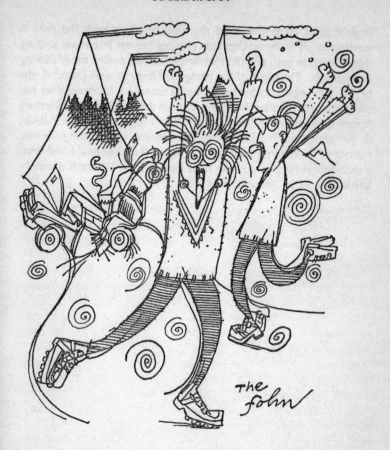

The fohn

and, pow, they let go. Time after time, I've noticed this very thing. They never hit anyone who is big and tough. Nor anyone who could use a nose job. So, upon my return to London I shall table a motion in Parliament asking for the abolition of the beef, and I hope the right honourable gentleman who is desperately trying to make bookie joints a better place to spend one's life in, will join me in sneaking it through.

After three weeks of sunshine, the dreaded *fohn*, the south wind that supposedly can drive men to murder and women to rape, arrived with a vengeance. Gstaad under cloudy skies and a hot southern wind can give one the *cafard*. Some people have been here since the beginning of December, and the altitude along with the *fohn* is starting to get to them. One lady crashed her car into mine, cutting mine almost in half, and then broke into sobs accusing me of driving dangerously. The night of the party for Diana R. and David B. she began, once again, to harangue me. It seems her husband does not allow her to ski because he thinks some of the local heroes will seduce her on some out-of-the-way slope. When I suggested to her that she do just that, and that it was the best antidote against the *fohn*, she ran out of the chalet screaming. Yet again, it looked as if I had been a cad, but nothing could have been further from the truth. I simply know what to do when the *fohn* hits.

· Spring fever ·

New York · Spring is here, which means a lot of tarts with new money and even newer faces will be trekking north from Palm Beach and other such southern playgrounds of bad taste. The arrival of people who kiss each other on both cheeks every time they meet one another is probably the only thing I have against spring. That and hay fever, needless to say.

Not that I have anything against Palm Beach as a resort. In fact, I used to love going there before Yoko Ono and others of her ilk discovered the place. It was in Palm Beach where a then recent acquaintance gave a ride in his brand new Rolls to a girlfriend of mine and myself, and – being a vulgarian – tried to impress my girl by asking if she had ever been in a Rolls before. 'Yes, but never in the front seat,' was her answer, and for some strange reason the acquaintance remained just that.

It was also in Palm Beach that I met a poor old Brit by the name of Cecil Everley. Cecil was a terribly nice man who had once supplemented his income by working as a gentleman's gentleman for a renowned and unacceptably rich old queen. After the queen's untimely death, Cecil moved to the better places on this earth, and while in Palm Beach had the bad luck to be introduced to the venom-tongued Daisy Fellows. She had just sold her yacht, the *Sister Anne*, and Cecil, trying to make polite conversation, asked her if she missed it. 'No, do you miss your tray?' came the rude answer. Cecil moved to the Côte d'Azur, I believe, the following day.

The last time I was in Palm Beach was just after the birth of my daughter and, such was the shock of fatherhood, I went down in order to recover. The place, however, had changed. Rich Europeans with athletic pretensions had moved in, along with Yoko, a dope-dealer or two, plus every unemployed prince this side of Andorra. The place was hell. The American old guard, as those duffers like to call themselves, were putting the wagons around their vulgar houses trying to keep out the Indians. The Indians, some of them European royals, others just simple rich folk like Yoko, as well as the drug-dealers, were busy putting their wagons up in an effort to keep out the old guard. It was pretty funny but hardly conducive to having a good time.

While I was down there the talk was about who among the Indians would be allowed to enter the clubs of Palm Beach. Both the Everglades and Bath and Tennis have strict rules about such important things as one's religion, ability to speak with one's mouth closed, and other such typically American *soi disant* upper-class give-aways. An old friend of mine, a man born under a somewhat more eastern sun than the one over France, one Robert de Balkany (the christian name was his at birth) had just moved to Palm Beach and apparently had made the mistake of trying to get into the B and T. I knew a big shot of the club and told him that Balkany might be a bit loud at times, but was not such a bad fellow after all. That he would be an asset to the place. And even went further by recounting a true story about Robert. I told the story assuming that the big shot – a real womanizer and knee-grabber if ever there was one – would appreciate the similar quality in Robert. How wrong I was. But first the story.

It was during 1968, when Paris had no petrol and the 'students' were on an ego trip while the world's press reported it as assiduously as they report American war games in Central America. We were all gathered at a house outside Paris when Robert offered to give a ride to a lady who lived at least five miles away and who was preparing to walk home. 'No thanks, Robert,' said she. 'I'm much too tired, I'd rather walk.'

Well, I don't know what happened to Balkany, if he got in or not, but I do know that I was trying to help him by telling the story. All these snobs, needless to say, will be here immediately after Easter, and that is why I am flying out next week.

· Status quo ·

Los Angeles · The last time I was in the city of angels was in 1972. I had just finished a three-month stint in Vietnam, and thought a week's rest and relaxation in the city that makes every cliché come true might be good for me. That was the year that a trained seal called Warren Beatty decided he should become the sexual symbol behind the White House and was fund-raising for McGovern. Now, 12 years later, the trained seal is at it again. This time he's campaigning for Gary Heartpenny. But I'm getting away from my story, which is about Los Angeles, and not about a radical-chic trained seal who thinks he understands politics.

I flew out here in order to tape a television show in conjunction with my nuclear physics book. The publishers had me billeted in the Beverly Hills Hotel, a place that even a sybarite like Farouk of Egypt would find posh. It is also the place where Anthony Haden-Guest is thought of as the epitome of England's aristocrats, and Charles Benson as a multi-millionaire. (They even think that Sebastian Taylor went to an English public school.) Well, I'm not surprised. I'd believe that Benson is a millionaire too if I lived in a city that calls used cars 'experienced' and garbage-collectors 'sanitary engineers'.

Although I had been to El Lay twice before, I had forgotten that walking in the city is akin to streaking during Trooping the Colour. Simply not done. People drive across the street, and Beverly Hills has 'valet' parking everywhere. (This service is performed by people who have not as yet made it in the flicks, and who park your car as you pull up. For a price, of course.) Status is what Hollywood is all about, and everywhere one looks there are status symbols to remind one that the rat-race is on. I saw kids driving to school in their BMWs and Mercedes, and heard a major movie mogul castigate a newly arrived hack for saying he 'had lunch', rather than the accepted 'did lunch'. Needless to say, the greatest status symbol is the home, as they call a house out here. One simply never buys just a home. One buys somebody's former home. The same applies to dentists. One doesn't go to any dentist. One goes to Jack's, Burt's, or Liza's.

Ditto where tonsorial parlours are concerned. Even stock brokerage firms.

The most important people in Hollywood and its environs are the head waiters of the few chic restaurants that do not serve macrobiotic food. The head waiters wield more power than any movie biggie by having the final word on the ultimate status symbol, the luncheon table. A good table means more in Hollywood than talent, money, looks, or – God forbid – intelligence. In the inferno of unrelenting egos that is lotus-land, a bad table is commensurate with a social death sentence. There is Morton's, Ma Maison, Chasen's and The Bistro. My first night I went to Morton's, where the Greek head waiter greeted me like a long-lost brother. 'I need to talk to you,' he whispered to me in our native language. 'Nobody here speaks because they're afraid they might get wrinkles around the mouth.'

When I rang Jon Bradshaw, a writer friend of mine, I was told he was hard at work. Bradshaw has been working on a book about a blues singer for seven years now. A film is about to be released of the blues singer's life. After the titles there is a notice, 'Soon to be a major book'. Talk about lotus-eaters, there are none. Lotuses, that is. The writers who come out here to work have eaten them all.

Writers who are too incompetent to make a living in London or New York are reduced to earning £150,000 a year in Hollywood writing 'treatments'. Screen-writers watch TV movies and then sit down and write variations on the theme of what they have seen. Once upon a time writers in Hollywood actually got their inspiration from reading books. A friend of mine told me that writers in New York turn into cockroaches, which at least survive – in Los Angeles they turn into avocados and rot.

Still, without the people it would be a hell of a place. A very clean place, I may add. Throw a paper hanky out of your Rolls, and you can get a $1,000 fine. I worked out that the sprinkling system of Los Angeles is worth more than the oil deposits off its coast. Much more, in fact. And if it weren't for the tall hedges that keep pools apart, I could have swum from one end of Beverly Hills to the other. And that is what the people do all day. Swim in their pools. When Bradshaw showed me the 7,000 words he had written in seven years, while lazing around his pool, I rushed to the airport. Three days in Beverly Hills could make a sybarite of me, too.

· Friend in need ·

The last time my friend Charles Benson was rich enough to have me to dinner was exactly ten years ago. For anyone unfamiliar with Lord Whelks's premier scout of the Turf, here is a brief résumé of his colourful life. Benson first became known when, fresh out of my old school, he was posted as the hottest favourite to commit suicide in Aspinall's old club – which proved how naïve even Aspers was back in those good old days, because Benson was as likely to commit *seppuku* over loss of face to the bookies he owed thousands to as, say, Gaddafi is ready to extradite the St James's Square murderer.

This was in the early Sixties. By the early Seventies Benson was a hunted man, emerging from a friend's flat only at night, sleeping in a different place every night, changing girls as often as I change friends, and spending his time studying brochures of far-away tropical places. The bookies, you see, were finally after him, and hanging around Benson was as dangerous as being an American Intelligence officer in Greece. After all, bookies have been known to remove the kneecaps of the wrong people more often than Nigel Dempster has been refused entrance to Annabel's, or Sebastian Taylor has been blackballed at White's. Despite the inherent dangers, however, I stuck by Benson, dining and gambling with him, at times even venturing out in broad daylight in his company.

And for once I was not disappointed. When Benson struck it rich, the last person he thought of paying was me. (If he had, I would have had a heart attack.) How did he do it? Easy. In 1974 Dunhill sponsored a backgammon tournament that was to be held on board the *QE2*, for the 32 best players in the world, with a first prize of $100,000. Now, Benson was not among the first 32, his religion was all wrong for that, nor was I, not having learned to cheat in my youth, but he somehow convinced the sponsors to include us on board.

I shall always remember that trip because (a) it cured me of any nostalgia I had for transatlantic voyages and (b) it gave me the opportunity to think of raising a family once Benson became financially independent. I got over my nostalgia for sea travel because the

QE2 was as terrible a ship as I had ever been on. The food and service were from the past, and by that I mean the kind of food they served to immigrants on steerage around the turn of the century. The service, ditto. Benson, needless to say, came through. He won the first prize the night before we landed in Southampton. The gambling world being what it is, news was leaked, and by the time we steamed in, there were more than 2,000 bookies waiting on the dockside. Benson immediately got the message and disappeared, disguising himself as a nanny (an old trick taught to him by a Turf Club lady-member, one Erica Nielsen), leaving me to deal with the motliest group of people this side of Samoa. The last thing I remember saying before being overwhelmed was, 'Gentlemen, you shall all be paid in due course.'

As I said, that was back in 1974. Benson paid some of the bookies, got his two boys out of hock (I swear he had pawned them both to a childless couple) and then proceeded to get married. As a wedding present I decided to forget past accounts. Benson was furious. He accused me of being Greek and mercenary.

Why am I dredging up past history? Because ten years after his first stroke of luck, the lady's lightning has once again struck Benson. About a month ago, he won over £300,000, and this time, in order to make amends, had me to dinner at his new palatial house near Kensington Palace. He even produced some royals to make me feel more at home, two Jordanian princesses and one Jordanian prince. Jordan is one of the few Arab countries I approve of, and its royal family the only one that has any balls. I must confess Benson's invitation moved me tremendously – so much, in fact, that I didn't mind when Benson's wife asked me to clear the table afterwards. (If anyone is stupid enough to serve me, a Greek, Mouton Rothschild '47, instead of retsina, his wife is right to try and get something back.)

The next night, the Jordanian royals had me to dinner and that turned out to be one of my best nights in London. As I write this, I am about to fly away to New York once again, this time for one month only. I am returning to play in a tennis tournament, and predict that by the time I'm back Benson will be, once again, Benson – i.e. broke and in debt to the bookies.

· Gross profits ·

Southampton, Long Island · The Hamptons were once a series of quiet, tiny, tranquil villages by the sea that served as a country refuge for New York City's rich. When I say rich, however, I mean those among the privileged who wished to live a quiet life by the sea, away from the hustle and bustle of Old Westbury, or Locust Valley, where the Jay Gatsbys of this world went hunting for social acceptance as soon as they had made their pile. The rich who preferred the Hamptons built vast frame houses, surrounded them with long green lawns, dotted the lawns with yellow-and-white umbrellas and wicker chairs, and planted stately maple trees and tall hedges to shield them from the not so rich. Everything was hunky-dory, as they say, until the politicians decided that the only way to get votes was to take from the rich and give it to the poor – in exchange for the latter's support. They called this unique system of robbery, taxation.

Needless to say, the rich survived. What they did was cut back on their lawns and the size of their houses. The panicky ones among them sold parts of their lawns to speculators, who in turn cut the 'property' up some more and sold it for vast profits. Before the Swinging Sixties had even begun to swing, the Hamptons were full of people who would have been too vulgar even in Los Angeles. (Incidentally, a bleached, middle-aged blonde by the name of Jean Valelly devoted a full-page column in the *Los Angeles Herald Examiner* to attack me for having written that El Lay is a place full of phoney blondes, trained seals and people without class. My dear Miss Vanilla, it is not only poor little me who says so. Walter Winchell said it was a place that shot movies instead of actors and actresses, while Raymond Chandler called it a city with the personality of a paper cup. I only said that there are as many good restaurants in El Lay as there are good writers in Hollywood.)

Well, as you might have guessed, the tranquil villages are no more. In the summer, that is – when the Hollywood crowd moves in. Do you believe that across from the stately Meadow Club lives Mr Woody Allen? That three blocks away from the exclusive Beach Club lives a Hollywood biggie called Barrish, a man so vulgar he's had trouble getting a table even in Ma Maison. Worse, on a typical summer weekend, herds of gaudily dressed day trippers swarm along the Hamptons' streets, and joggers sweat, grunt and wheeze along every avenue and strip of grass.

Needless to say, the few great estates that have not been broken down by greedy speculators, have been bought by what are known over here as greenmailers. These are people who are mostly fat and bald, and who buy large amounts of stock in a company, spread rumours that they are about to take it over by offering much more per share, and when the stock shoots up, either sell what they already own at a great profit, or take over the company and strip it of its assets and sell them for vast gains. The Hamptons, for some strange reason, are full of greenmailers of late. They drive around in white Rolls Royces, give large luncheons every Saturday, and instruct their press agents to give away their list of invitees to the gossip columns. Although old-time residents of the Hamptons look upon these vulgarians in a way not unlike that in which the Kremlin looks upon democrats, unlike the Kremlin, there is not much they can do about the invasion of the body snatchers, as a local wit described the greenmailers.

What does all this mean? It means that the old guard has something more to talk about than the weather, or who has boffed whose wife. In fact, there is a plethora of subjects that can be judged safe enough to talk about this spring. The latest has nothing to do with houses, it has to do with ... a book. But before I mislead you, no, it is not a book about ideas, but about the Kennedys. This one has been written by Jackie K.O's first cousin, a professional writer named John Davis. It is a serious study of the Kennedys and it reveals certain, shall I say, weaknesses in their character. The revelation that has everyone laughing is the one concerning Jackie's mother, Janet Lee, Bouvier, Auchincloss, and yet another name I can't remember. It is alleged that Jackie's mother went as far as telling everyone who toured her house – Hammersmith Farm, or the Summer White House, as she liked to call it – that she was descended from the Lees of Virginia. As Jackie's cousin points out, nothing is further from the truth. Janet Lee was as Irish as blarney and the shamrock. Her father was an Irish immigrant who made good and married her off to the poor Bouvier fellow. But not to worry. If you don't find these revelations earth-shattering, it only means that you won't fit in the Hamptons scene.

· Poetry ·

Listening to the harangues at the Democratic convention in San Francisco reminded me of those mobs that harangued the crowds 196 years ago in Paris. Either I am out of touch with reality, or the haranguers are completely out of touch with the people they purport to speak for. Just consider the following: Governor Cuomo of New York belts out that Ronald Reagan does not care about the abject poor, the unemployed, or the disenfranchised but cares only for his (Reagan's) 'hysterical commitment to an arms race that leads nowhere', and the press and the floor go wild for days over the greatest speech since the Gettysburg address. The fact that unemployment was 18.8 per cent when Reagan took office and today it is around 10.6 per cent is judged immaterial.

The *capo di tutti capi* of New York, however, was not the most brazen. Jesse Jackson and the lady from Queens (and I don't mean the tennis club) are the ones who established an atmosphere of hatred unheard of in American politics. Jackson's speech was predictably too long, too loud, and much too theatrical. The response of the faithful was to burst out crying. The TV cameras kept zooming in, focusing on the tears, and the only thing that struck me was how truly ugly most of the delegates were. And overweight. And hysterical. And how the press manipulated them by zooming in on them with their cameras and how they responded by raising the decibel levels even higher. Pavlov would have cried in shame.

I almost cried with frustration at what has happened to the Democratic Party of Harry Truman and J. F. Kennedy, but finally I decided it wasn't worth it. (I've already seen much the same happen right here, to the Labour Party) – especially after seeing that distinguished literary figure, one Leroi Jones, a.k.a. Amiri Baraka (if he's a true poet, I'm a teetotalling, drug-free virgin), scream: 'You're a whore, Andy, you're a whore. No, you're not even a whore, you're worse,' at Andrew Young for supporting Walter Mondale. So, taking the advice of Mr Anthony Trollope – who described San Francisco as the least interesting city he had ever visited in his travels – I decided I'd rather be in Philadelphia.

One night in the city of brotherly love and then it was up to Southampton for the annual George Plimpton bash last Sunday. Plimpton's house is right on the ocean and has an enormous lawn at the back where the baseball game takes place. Unfortunately, most of George's friends are liberals, so when I wasn't taking batting practice I chatted with my other friend, Bob Hughes, the art critic. Bob was sad about the death of James Fixx, the man who spurred the jogging craze with his best-selling books about running, and puzzled as well. 'Here I am,' he told me, 'a boozer who never takes exercise but is still around, and Fixx is dead.' 'Write something about the irony of it,' someone told him, and the Aussie sat right down in front of me and in ten minutes wrote the following:

> *The Glutton, gross in paunch and thigh,*
> *Eludes the Reaper grim:*
> *Swollen of nose, and pink of eye,*
> *The Drunkard laughs at him.*
>
> *The chairbound Journalist, the Don,*
> *Carelessly quaff champagne,*
> *The Pop-Star lives for ever, on*
> *Pills, bimbos, and cocaine.*
>
> *Frustrated by this doleful news,*
> *DEATH newer victims picks,*
> *He laces on his jogging-shoes,*
> *And catches up with FIXX.*

Well, it ain't Keats but it's good enough for me. So good, in fact, that once again I overdid it over the weekend and when I landed back in London I was finally invited by the Queen to be her guest. I guess it was about time. I'd been angling for an invitation for ages.

· Docked ·

The cruellest blow of all was dealt to me last weekend. There I was looking forward to one more week of debauchery and decadence when the telephone rang and it was obvious that it was bad news the moment I picked it up. It was the mother of my children, ringing to announce her imminent arrival – with my children – in order to lend moral support at my impending trial – which, by the way, will be more infamous than the one that sent Ireland's greatest playwright to prison for buggery, or whatever excuse it was they found to send poor Oscar down. My solicitor, in the meantime, keeps warning me not to be a smart alec while in the dock. (Remember F. E. Smith? 'There he was, drunk as a judge,' said Lord Birkenhead while testifying in court. 'You mean drunk as a lord,' interrupted the judge. 'Yes, my Lord,' said Birkenhead, and the man in whose favour he was testifying went down.) My solicitor also reminds me of Oscar Wilde's arrogance in court, and how in the end it did him in. (Mr Carson: 'Do you drink champagne yourself?' Oscar Wilde: 'Yes. Iced champagne is a favourite drink of mine – strongly against my doctor's orders.' Mr Carson: 'Never mind your doctor's orders, sir.' Oscar Wilde: 'I never do.')

Of course, none of these remarks were as bad as the one that I personally heard a friend of mine come up with when he appeared before an American judge for drunken driving, resisting arrest, and biting the arresting officer's ear. When the judge asked him if this was the first time he was up before him, my friend couldn't resist the following: 'I don't know, your Honour, what time did you get up this morning?' He got six months.

The most ridiculous reason for going to jail that I know of happened to yet another friend of mine in Monte Carlo. He and I were very drunk and decided to relieve ourselves in front of the casino. When the fuzz arrived I resisted a bit and then went along to the police station. While I was resisting, my friend continued to relieve himself on the leg of the officer who had a headlock on me. Needless to say, once they had the cuffs on me they turned their clubs on him and there was nothing I could do to help him as by then I had been tied to a tree. Worse, when they got us to the station, my friend announced in a loud voice that he and Princess Grace had been extremely intimate while she lived in Philadelphia. Despite my assurances that he was only joking, the KGB-like Monaco cops went to work on him. The next day I was allowed to go back to Antibes with a warning not to use the sacred soil of Monte Carlo as a *pissoir*, or else – while my poor buddy had to spend one week incommunicado before being thrown out of the Principality for good. (Little did we realize how lucky we were at the time. Being thrown out of Monte is as bad as not being allowed into Beirut.)

Well, I know all this sounds a bit sordid, but what am I to do? I am certainly not about to cry, and if I am sent down it will only bring back happy memories of my Eton days. Which reminds me, I have to put my young son down for my old Alma Mater before it's too late. When I heard my children speak I almost fainted. Their accent is so American they make me sound like someone Heath would like to sound like if he could get the word house right.

Needless to say, the last weekend was spent in Wiltshire among children, dogs, wives, friends, and even a film actress. My children have not been told that their father might be taking yet another trip, so fortunately they left me alone with my thoughts of enforced solitude. My landlady must have suspected something because she had me and the wife for dinner every day. Her two daughters, too, were extremely nice to me for a change – as was the mother of my *Kinder*. Amazing what a little time in the clink will do for one's popularity. The only bad taste was shown by my mistress, who refused to come and see me while my wife was around, and even went as far as to threaten to leave me in case I went to prison. As my old daddy always told me, never trust a girl who is less than half your age. What he should have warned me about was aristocratic crumpet that will not wait two or three months while I pay my debt to café society. I guess that's why I think I'll stick to my wife. After all, she's older and more patient. And, knowing how narrow-minded prison guards are, I imagine a mistress would be no good for a visit.

· Snags ·

To say that I've hit a snag in the pursuit of the high life would be an understatement. The morbid fascination with self-destruction has also come to a halt. Suddenly one wants serenity and balance but both are for the moment inaccessible. After three weeks of ups and downs, it has suddenly dawned on me that things will never be the same again. Well, the only thing that makes it easier for me to bear the public humiliation is the fact that I have no one to blame but myself. In my experience there are those who express their impotence in aggression, and there are others who convey it through self-denigration. Throughout my life I've always been aggressive when down. This time, although I can't bear self-loathing, I am not about to go around celebrating and hitting people. Some of my friends think that the literary flame might be kindled by all this, but I doubt it. I need to be arrogant to be good, and I ain't feeling arrogant right now. What I am feeling is humble, with a little help from Customs and Excise, of course.

What I find interesting, however, is the fact that living recklessly in the fast lane does not necessarily mean that when one crashes one's troubles are over. More often than not one is maimed for life, and spends the rest of one's life regretting. The best examples I know are my two maternal uncles. One of them was the most brilliant lawyer in Greece, but by the age of 30 he was paralysed from his neck down, and today, 40 years later, he is a shell of a man, bedridden for 40 years all because of one moment of folly. A German officer had bet him he wouldn't jump from a particular cliff which was just not high enough for a parachute to open. My uncle Nicholas took him up on it as if national honour was at stake.

My other uncle was even crazier. When he was 12 years old he wrote Mussolini a letter and got himself invited as the Duce's guest to Villa Borghese for one month. When the Italo-Greek war broke out he distinguished himself by being awarded the highest decoration Greece had to offer. Throughout four years of German occupation he fought in the mountains, and then continued to fight the communists until the civil war was over. He was extremely good-looking and probably the randiest man in that randiest of countries. He was also always in love. When peace came he got bored. When a fellow officer went after his girl he challenged him to a game of Russian roulette – and lost.

Well, if it sounds pretty useless, it was. But there is some consolation. I don't think my uncle Taki would have liked the present world, so maybe he knew something the rest of us don't. Yes, I guess one moment of impulse can change one's life for ever. Take the case of another friend of mine, Pierre Mairesse Le Brun. It was in 1968 and the *soi disant* students had brought Paris to a halt. All sporting events were called off in case it made the ruling class look as if it were amusing itself. Even the polo was called off, which made all of us extremely angry with the students as well as the gutless people who ran the polo. In order to retaliate we had a large party at the polo club and, with black tie, and very drunk, drew up sides for a moonlit game. Pierre Mairesse, who had been a cavalry officer and had been wounded badly during the war, asked to be tied on his horse, and sure enough he was (he was too drunk to stay on otherwise). The game was fun for a while, with people falling off and girls running on the field, until Pierre's horse fell and rolled over him. He broke his neck and has been partly paralysed ever since. I was among those who had had the brilliant idea to have the game, and perhaps one of the reasons I stopped polo and Paris soon after was because of that night. (1968 was a horrid year. One week later, in a practice match, Elie de Rothschild lost his eye when a ball struck him.)

I've had a lot of time to think back these past three weeks, and I must admit I've dodged my share of bullets. In fact, last winter my wife threw out a handgun I kept in New York when, drunk one night, I began challenging another clown who had stayed up with me. Just as well, too. With my luck, I probably would have missed myself, hit him and been charged with murder.

· Truman ·

I've rarely heard Gianni Agnelli, that most charismatic and charming of men, sound sadder over the telephone. We spoke last Sunday and it was the chairman of Fiat who informed me of Truman Capote's death. Gianni is no humbug. He had every right to feel sad. After all, he was among the few of Truman's powerful friends who didn't turn against him after excerpts of the most famous unfinished work appeared in *Esquire* about eight years ago. The excerpts aroused a furore among the rich and privileged because many of them thought they recognized themselves in the book's scandalous chronicle of their life. Well, all I can say is that it was the other way round. The ones who howled the loudest were the ones who could not recognize themselves, however hard they tried. Ironically, the three main characters were composites of Babe Paley, Anne Woodward, and Nelson Rockefeller, none of whom made too much of what was called by the parasites among them the betrayal of the century.

I remember the furore well. Truman had made it very clear that he felt his only capital was his past experience of life. And that resenting the fact that a writer dips into his assets was like resenting the fact that a rich man spends his money. (Just as ironically, most of his rich critics were the type known in France as *vivre à droite et voter à gauche*.)

Needless to say, Capote didn't mind at all about his *soi disant* loss of friends among the rich and famous. It was the press that played that particular angle up. Well, all I can say is it was par for the course. After all, what else is the press good for except to get it wrong where writing is concerned. The unkindest cut of all, I thought, was that in later years Capote was always portrayed as a man who turned to drink and dope following the closing of ranks by the very rich. All I can say to that is a composite word not suited to appear in the *Spectator* except in the column immediately following mine. Capote, like most writers in general, and southern American writers in particular, drank and doped from the start.

His earliest novel, *Other Voices, Other Rooms*, and many of his short stories were in the mainstream of southern literature – a haunted narrative poem about a boy moving through a Gothic childhood. (The American South produces writers writing about the tortures of childhood like California produces tennis players and hippies.) And his childhood was certainly a Gothic tale of terror. His mother locked him up in a room for long periods and made it clear to him that she loathed him. She later committed suicide, after divorcing his father. I guess it doesn't take a $1,000-per-hour Beverly Hills shrink to see that perhaps his childhood had something to do with his self-destructive streak once he had become famous.

And famous – as well as extremely bitchy – he was. After I had got into trouble recently he rang me and assured me that it would all blow over one day. I wasn't so sure – and still am not – but he insisted that the writing is what lasts. Not the scandals. I only hope he was right. Which he was most of the time. As far as I'm concerned, in fact, Truman should be appreciated by lovers of books if only for his definition of the stream of consciousness way of novel-writing. 'It's typing, not writing,' was the way he explained the phenomenon during its heyday in the early Sixties.

His bitchiness, of course, was legendary. When David Susskind, a nice man, interviewed him on television and indiscreetly asked him if he had ever made love to a woman, Truman declined to answer. But afterwards, at Elaine's with 20 pairs of indiscreet ears listening, he told us how the only woman he had ever made love to was Mrs David Susskind. His fights with Gore Vidal and Norman Mailer I always suspected were not for real, although he did remark once that the only thing wrong with Gore is the fact that he goes to sleazy massage parlours. He was a *farceur*, but not a poseur, and he saw through most of the humbug in today's revolting world. When I spoke to him about the mess I'd got myself into, he told me about the Ferraro woman, and how phoney she is. It seems that she was known as Mrs Zaccaro until 1978, when she first ran and was elected to Congress. She changed her name because she knew that Zaccaro meant slum dwellings and low dealings, not because – as the media believe – she wanted to honour her mother and father. Truman knew, because he, too, had changed his name. And for the same reason as Ferraro. Shame for his family.

· Dynasty ·

Their story could have made every Hollywood hack weep with envy. It is set against all the glamour the latter part of the 20th century can muster. Theirs is also a simple love story. One beautiful princess falls in love, and despite her parents' objections and her court responsibilities, she marries him. Love conquers all. Fade out, cut and print.

The sister, too, falls in love with a racing driver whose father is France's most popular star. Her father approves. But suddenly she falls in love with another, whose father is also a great star, but who is *persona non grata* with her father. But love wins out yet again. She stays with the black sheep, the jailbird. Cut and print.

Well, not quite. As everyone who has ever been ripped off in Monte Carlo knows, I'm talking about Caroline and Stephanie Grimaldi, better known as the girls who made the French magazine *Paris Match* a going concern by appearing on its cover more often than Princess Diana has gone on shopping sprees. (Apparently *Match* was doing rather badly until they decided to assign a hack and five paparazzi to shadow les girls of the late Grace Kelly and never let them out of the sight of their zoom lenses.) As it turns out, this has led to the start of a cold war between the Palace of Monaco and the Fourth Estate of the nation that once relied on the *ligne Maginot* to keep trespassers out.

But the French press refuses to give the Mrs Miniver-type of image to the Grimaldi girls. Instead, they are depicted as ladies who simply just can't help it – running around with the wrong boys, that is. Caroline started the rot by marrying Philip Junot, a man I know well. I suspect even hookers in the bar of the Hôtel de Paris were appalled to hear she was about to marry him. After spending most of their time in various nightclubs, Caroline and Junot broke up, but not before tarnishing the already soiled image of Monaco. After the break-up Caroline remained in the headlines, as well as on the cover of *Paris Match* (Monte Carlo Match, would be a more appropriate name), by going out with a tennis star, a punk rocker, a minor playboy, and finally a man whose background would not be considered aristocratic even in Albania. The fact that she married him while five months pregnant didn't help. The Italian she married made sure he got his fair share of publicity by attacking anyone and everyone within range who was in possession of a camera.

But just as the public seemed to tire of the common Italian and the half-Irish, half-Mediterranean princess, in stepped her younger

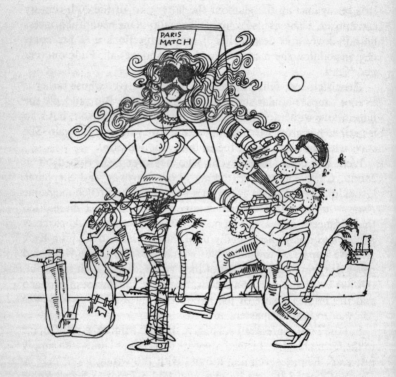

sister. Stephanie is not as pretty as Caroline, but she makes up for it by being more open about her love life. After being unofficially engaged to the son of Jean Paul Belmondo, she left him suddenly for the son of Alain Delon, a boy who has already been convicted of stealing a car, possessing a gun, and beating up a policeman. (He is 18.)

Needless to say, *Match* and the rest of the French papers had a field day. The Grimaldis tried to stop any pictures of the couple appearing in print – unsuccessfully I may add – when they should have simply stopped Stephanie from making a fool of herself in public. Which brings me to the point of my story. Here is a joke state, run by an absolute monarch (mind you, a benevolent one) whose welfare is based on dreams, illusions and tax shelters, but whose main concern is trying to stop the press from writing about the royal lowness of the ruling family. Even Albert, Rainier's heir, and a man who should know better having gone to an American university, is guilty of the same thing. I've sat next to him and seen him threaten photographers who took his picture. Where were we? Why, in a seedy nightclub, of course, where else?

But not to worry. The press gives as good as it gets. By publishing the shenanigans of the Grimaldis it has upped its circulation by ten per cent. In fact, so successful has any Monte Carlo story been in financial terms, people come over simply for the publicity. The latest buffoon to fly over from America was Jesse Jackson, the irreverent clown who wants to be president. He got the publicity he wanted but he failed to surprise anyone in Monte. He fitted in perfectly.

· Dining out ·

I don't know why, but everything about Princess Michael of Kent rubs me the wrong way. Perhaps it is because most of the pushy types I know – and I know too many – are short (Sebastian Taylor, the Wildenstein family, Yoko Ono, etc.) and she is over six feet tall. Or maybe it is because she's Austrian and my noble Austrian relatives (through marriage, alas) snigger when her name pops up. (Her father was as much a baron, it seems, as Kagan was a peer before Harold Wilson.) And then it may be that I take the word of David Linley (a man I don't know but whose taste in ladies like Cosima Fry I approve), who said that nothing could be worse than dining with the Valkyrian-built blonde.

Well, no. There is something worse, and that is dining with Linley's mother. Last spring, in New York, I was invited to dinner with PM and neither she nor I distinguished ourselves terribly that night. Although I cannot repeat private conversations, for the sake of the few gossips that read the *Spectator* I must at least give a hint. Most of the conversation had to do with, yes, you guessed it, Princess Michael of Kent. I was seated at the other end and only caught snatches, but it was enough. When Princess Margaret got up to leave she sort of stood next to me for a moment while I searched for words (mind you, I was already quite drunk). 'Do you remember when we met in 1967?' I ventured. Although my speech was slightly slurred, I nevertheless didn't realize how inarticulate I was being until I heard her Highness's reply. 'What, you're a civil servant?' she snapped. 'No, I asked if you remember meeting in '67,' I tried again. 'You *are* a civil servant,' came the reply once again. That is when I gave up and asked her, 'Excuse me, Ma'am, but do I look like a civil servant?' Unfortunately, I never found out. PM was about to answer me when the black piano player at Mortimer's – who didn't know any better, poor boy – started playing 'God Save the Queen'. As soon as she heard that, I swear PM forgot all about my profession and plunked herself down. Then I really went too far. Sitting – or standing, rather – next to me was Jerry, a White House visitor and a man of whom many things have been said but never that he was too masculine. I couldn't resist the slur, so I put my two cents in: 'Don't worry, it's not for you, Ma'am, it's for Jerry.'

Needless to say, I have not had any meals either with royals or with Jerry lately, and for once I'm not surprised. After all, if everyone began making jokes while out with royals, this country would end up being the kind Scargill and his ilk would like it to be; thus I am the first to appreciate what royals stand for. But now it seems that soon I may be dining with royals again. I have heard that Princess Michael is going on the lecture circuit, charging £2,000 per speech, not an excessive amount if one takes into account that in America criminal drug-dealers (like one caught *in flagrante* trying to sell three kilos of cocaine) actually demand and get $5,000 to lecture to students in universities.

What will the Princess talk about? If she's smart, and she is, she will tell the fat cats she'll be addressing how private enterprise helped her get a foothold on the red carpet. Most of them will be self-made people and will love it. But I'm afraid that she won't. She will probably talk about her Austrian background, and all about Vienna's influence in civilizing Europe, a true enough fact but the wrong subject for self-made men to have to listen to.

I can almost hear it: 'Accept your position with the blithe air of entitlement that only hereditary queens (monarchs, rather) are capable of. Do not grasp at those little validations, dignities, and reassurances that affirm one's station in life ...' It would be a great speech and she would be great in giving it. Alas, it will not take place. And it's a pity. If Princess Michael took herself a bit less seriously she would be much more popular, especially, I suspect, with those she wants desperately to impress, her royal cousins through marriage.

· Time out ·

By the time you read this, I will most likely be taking my first (however enforced) holiday from the *Spectator* after a run of 372 weeks. Without meaning to brag, I thought it was about time I drew attention to the fact. After all, the gutter press – oblivious to the truth as usual – have labelled me a playboy, forgetting the days, weeks, even months that Auberon Waugh, the sainted editor, the ex-sainted ex-editor, and even Jeffrey Bernard take off each year.

Well, I will let the *Spectator* readers decide who the playboys are among us. After 372 weeks of hard labour I can honestly say that only two of my columns have failed to appear, and not because I was in Languedoc, or in Tuscany, or even Memphis, but simply because someone deemed them too nice. Which leads me to suspect that it will be strange suddenly not to be writing the columns. Perhaps not as strange as the place I'll be at, if the worst comes to the worst, but nevertheless rather abnormal.

Coming to the end of the writing of a column – for however brief a time – makes one want to summarize, to reach some kind of conclusion, to say something grand. The irony is that the more one tries to think of a conclusion, or of something on a grand scale, the more one realizes that it is something only fools or pompous left-wing American pundits do. Let's face it. Writing for the *Spectator* has been the thing that I've loved the most these last seven and a half years, my two *Kinder* and a woman or two naturally excluded.

So, why persevere with some kind of summing up? Self-importance, that's why. What is there to say? Not much, except that it still surprises me when I read that two Kennedys were arrested the other day for violating laws protecting foreign embassies in Washington while protesting against the apartheid system of South Africa. I say it surprises me because I think that by now they might have learned. Learned that at this moment the gravest human crisis on the African continent is being played out in Ethiopia, where the massive starvation was brought on by the policies of a black Marxist tyrant who took his lead from Stalin and used starvation as a political instrument.

Yet the Kennedy kids, like so many of those who think like they do, bang on about the only regime in Africa that one feels safe to attack any time, anywhere. No Kennedy child has as yet been arrested protesting about the genocidal war against Afghanistan, the persecution of the Catholic Church in Poland, or even the tyranny of the Kremlin over the Russian people. Not to mention the savagery

of the North Vietnamese over the South, or the fact that Libyans go around shooting people.

It is all a matter of priorities, but the trendies somehow never seem to understand it. They want to effect changes in Western policies toward South Africa, South Korea, El Salvador and Turkey, which they would never attempt to do where Bulgaria or Vietnam, let alone the Soviet Union, is concerned. Just imagine what people of the West would have done if an American right-winger had tried to shoot the Pope under orders from the CIA. Or better yet, just imagine what the press would say if South Korea financed its army by drug dealing, as the PLO partly does. Syria reportedly runs heroin laboratories, North Korean diplomats have been caught bringing narcotics into Europe, while the Bulgarians run guns into the Middle East in exchange for the drugs they move into Nato Europe, yet it's Turkish human rights we worry about.

I guess it's a mark of our moral flaccidity that we continue to maintain relations with governments that kill their enemies in our very own backyards, *à la* Zhivkov, and encourage the kind of show-boating the Kennedys and their apologists tend to adopt whenever their names drop out of print. And speaking of drugs and the Kennedys – I still have not managed to discover the difference – here are my parting thoughts on the subject. I have always believed that any apologist for them – the drugs, that is – should be locked up and the proverbial key thrown away. The fact that I got caught with some should not disqualify me from preaching or speaking out against them. On the contrary, in fact, like an old Marxist seeing the light and turning. The pushers and the drug apologists should be attacked, but so should governments who deal with regimes that openly ply the drug trade. Like Castro's Cuba, for example.

But I digress. When I was stopped at Heathrow my first reaction was what people like Charles Moore, Mary Kenny, Richard Sykes and Dick West would think. And, of course, my father. Ironically, all of them have been understanding, while it has been others – people who have spilled more happy dust than I've ever taken – who have dined out on my problems. But I will take the advice of my friend Anne Somerset and not name names. This should be a happy occasion. After all, I am finally about to take a long-needed holiday, and because of it I've even managed to get the Taki philosophy across. I hope to be back soon, and in the meanwhile I wish all of you a very happy Christmas.

1985

· Day after day ·

Throughout the past three months I have kept a diary, which, in view of the time I had on my hands, makes Proust's remembrances positively laconic. This was the first time that I had kept a journal figuring that recording my life while in prison would not be regarded by my peers as an act of great egotism and conceit. Nor could I be accused of self-indulgence by those who think that hanging around Annabel's every night is a waste of time and money. After all, I was the only prisoner who worked seven days a week while 1,200 other layabouts indulged in the work ethic only on five days.

Given the fact that the daily life of a prisoner is not exactly a bravura performance, half of my diary is action, the other half reflection. But before any of you start reaching for your pens in order to write and protest to the sainted one, let me assure you that *Spectator* readers will be spared the Taki journals. The reasons are obvious. My Proustian tale of incarceration, and my reflections on the human condition while wearing striped pyjamas have no place under a 'High life' heading, and no space either.

This, then, will be the first and probably the last time I shall write about my life in the nick on these hallowed pages, and I will do it by the time-honoured method of 'a day in the life' of Taki in Pentonville. It is probably the best way of telling any young readers that although prison is less boring than, say, hanging around the Coach and Horses with small-time criminals all day, it is not remotely as much fun as being the guest of the Beauforts at Badminton or the Agnellis at Vilar Perosa. Or even the Chancellors in Tuscany.

6.45 a.m. The officer (if you're an Eton man like myself) or the screw (if one is a borstal alumnus) flicks on the light from the outside of the cell and another day begins. By 7.30 I have made my bed, have shaved in the plastic bowl that I filled with water the night before, and am anxiously listening for the jingling of keys so I will be ready for slop-out. This process is exactly what it says. The trick is to hold one's breath, tip the potty, wash it, and run from the recess area with still enough oxygen in one's lungs to make it out of there. Most prisoners, however, do not bother with lung exercises. Some of them even use the lavatory area as a meeting place, chatting and laughing like tourists in the Piazza San Marco during carnival time.

By eight o'clock the various landings are being called down for breakfast. I take my plastic cup, plate and bowl and walk down to D-2 where there is porridge, tea and beans. Then it's back inside my cell, the door is slammed shut and I have the first of the three solitary meals of the day. And the first cigarette of the day. Prisoners roll their own, but I invested my weekly salary in buying them ready-made as I found the rolling process as tedious as prison itself. Pretty soon the anxious waiting for the jingling of the keys starts all over again. It's slop-out time once more, and this time one needs two trips to the nick's favourite meeting place. One to wash out the cup and bowl, the other for the potty. By nine o'clock, I feel as if I can swim the English Channel underwater, such is my lung capacity.

At 9 a.m. precisely all doors are unlocked and we head for the various workshops. Some go to number one shop, where they sew laundry bags, some to number two or three shop where they make army jackets, prison clothes and various other items needed for the sartorial splendour of the inmates. I head for the gym. Once there I give out plimsolls, vests and shorts to those who have chosen the healthy life, and sweep the showers and put away what I've given out as soon as the hour is up. I also take part in the basketball games, weight-lifting and boxing that are part of the day's activities.

By 11.30 everyone is back in their cells and dinner is served. There is mashed potatoes, cabbage, meat, tea and a sweet. It is not the Ritz, nor is it the Gulag. People like Charles Benson wouldn't touch it, but most prisoners aren't as spoilt as he is and certainly not as greedy. By 1.30 p.m. we have slopped out once again, and I am back in the gym, this time until 4.30. Just before that, I have taken my daily shower – the only one in the whole nick who has that privilege, others bathe once a week. Then I go down for 'tea'. Tea means potatoes, cabbage, some meat, tea and a sweet. Then we are banged up once again, until the final exercise of holding one's breath around six in the evening. It is now lock-up time until the next morning. I read my newspapers, write my diary, and study the things I should have learned in school 30 years ago. At around midnight I manage to fall asleep. My lights have been left on for as long as I want. It is Pentonville's greatest advantage. I dream of the high life, the one I will be reporting to you from Gstaad next week.

· In the club ·

Gstaad · The Eagle Club was founded in 1957 by dissident members of the Corviglia Club who had decided to move over to Gstaad from St Moritz. I say dissident because it sounds better than disenchanted, which those who moved over from the Engadine certainly were. In essence the ones who moved were not happy with the dictatorial methods of an extremely rich Greek member of the Corviglia committee who had the until then unheard of idea to insist that those who picked up most of the bills for the running of the club would make up most of the rules.

Although the dissidents were of the upper-class persuasion, once in Gstaad they quickly turned Marxist. The Eagle Club was founded on the Soviet model, with a central committee and an all-powerful president running the lives of its members. The first president was Lord Warwick, the only man I've ever met who drank a whisky sour every morning before his eggs and bacon. When my name was put up for membership, the since departed Fulke Warwick did a Niarchos and told the rest of the screaming members that Taki was born to be a member of the Eagle, and if they didn't like it (which they certainly didn't) they could all go back to St Moritz or whichever resort they had come from.

That was back in 1958. By 1960 I had managed to get suspended for a year for conduct unbecoming a skier – i.e. I had thrown a cake that hit the Aga Khan and also besmirched the Pucci blouse of the wife of a British ambassador to Berne. Warwick was understanding, however. 'My grandfather tried to burn a fellow member at White's,' he told me, 'and nothing ever came of that.' The second president, le Vicomte Benoist d'Azy, was even nicer to me. He allowed both my wife and girlfriend to come into the club without paying and pretended they were both Madame Taki. (The French have impeccable understanding about such matters, *n'est ce pas*?) When le Vicomte sadly died I knew my days would be numbered. So I tried a Papandreou and decided to run for the presidency myself. I even got about 40 members to vote for me, but then failed to show up for the ballot due to a hangover that would have kept even Jeffrey

Bernard from the Coach and Horses.

This proved to be a mistake. While I was paying my debt to society, a fat Belgian social climber saw his chance and began canvassing around to make Pentonville the only club I belong to. (Little did he know that I am also a member of White's and the Beefsteak.) But wiser heads prevailed. My friend Basil Goulandris, who unfortunately for him has known me all my life, did a Niarchos, and dismissed the matter outright. Others, less autarchic, and typically American, wrote notes defending me. The one I liked the best came from the pen of Professor John Kenneth Galbraith (whom I managed to insult because I agreed with his figures, unheard of where Galbraith and Taki are concerned). He wrote, and I quote, 'In view of the fact that 50 per cent of the Club's members belong behind bars, it would be unseemly to punish Taki.' The catch word is 'unseemly'. William F. Buckley was more charitable. He wrote about *malum prohibitum* and *malum per se* (or I think he did, as my Latin got a bit rusty in the nick); i.e. the former is as if I went through a red light and killed someone, while the latter is as if I went through a red light and smashed myself up. Which I did. The Belgian's bid to rid the Eagle of one of the few members who can count as well as read and write (Goulandris, Buckley, and Jack Hemingway being the others – Galbraith has refused to become a member but sent in his note anyway) turned out to be as successful as *la ligne Maginot* was against my great-uncle back in 1940, but that is not the point. Why, in my hour of need, intellectuals and Greeks (people whom I have waged war against for years) keep coming to my aid, is.

To top it off, another Goulandris, Aleco, gave a dinner where the only commoner attending was yours truly, and where I had the bad luck to meet a young man whose name is Schoenburg and who mistook me for my wife. 'Are you Schoenburg-Glochau, or Schoenburg-Hartenstein?' he lisped. 'Glochau you too,' I told him, and it's been the rudest thing I've said to anyone since coming out from Caledonian Road. The next night I went to the Ruspoli dinner where my friend Zographos began his old tricks of throwing pies on ladies with tiaras, but being on parole has its advantages. For once I refused to join in and was not accused of showing the kind of courage the French showed in the spring of 1940, and I went home without hearing the familiar sound of 'This man should be behind bars.'

· Handicapped ·

Finding something original to say about age is almost as hard as forgetting that age exists. Everyone, except for people who sit on top of poles in India, has somewhere along the line thought and worried about it. Last week I sat with one of the greatest all-round athletes of all time discussing the aches and pains that come with maturity. The conversation was so depressing that I finally decided to read out loud what the French poet Paul Claudel wrote in his journal concerning the ravages of age: 'No eyes left, no ears, no teeth, no legs, no wind. And how astonishingly well one does without them.'

Philippe Washer, once the premier tennis player in Europe, a golfing champion, Olympic skier and good amateur boxer, is unfortunate enough to be 15 years older than I am, thus feeling 15 times the pain I do after a rough day's skiing. Last week we took a helicopter ride and were deposited on top of a mountain that few goats would dare scale. A Swiss helicopter costs per minute what the Duke of Westminster collects per second in rents (the deal being that some skiers keep the chopper hovering above in case they get into trouble), so we told him to forget us, that we'd make it down on our own without a guide.

Well, the trouble we did get into. It took us six hours to get down a mountain that usually takes us 45 minutes. When we arrived I was white with fear and exhaustion, Philippe only with the latter. The snow had changed overnight and we kept breaking through. Then the fog arrived and we had to keep yelling at each other in order not to get lost. The worst moment came when Washer reminded me that if we fell in a crevasse our bodies would be perfectly preserved until some explorer from outer space eventually found us.

But that is not the point of the story. It is how tired we were the next day – days, rather. And how nervous one had felt at not being sure that one would be back in a comfortable Gstaad hotel that night. No wonder downhill skiers call it quits by the time they reach their late twenties. It's not the legs that go, but the heart. Back in 1958 I skied down a mountain that had only a net to catch the unfortunate skier who caught an edge. If you missed the net it was

O. A. PLAYBOY

goodbye. I was with Nicky Rommel, the Fieldmarshal's nephew, and an English girl, Caroline Townsend. We had to get on a tiny ledge over a precipice to put the skis on. I told Rommel that with his heroic name he should carry the girl's skis out on the ledge. But she wouldn't have it, being English and all that. So I made him carry mine as he had been out on that ledge before, and while I was putting my skis on Caroline fell. The net came up trumps, however, but only thinking about it today makes me nervous, whereas I remember going up and doing that same mountain the next day and Rommel not having to carry my skis either.

First goes the heart, then the legs, finally the looks. An old athlete even looks scared. What is worse is that there are few athletes with enough intellect to fall back on once their playing days are over. This might sound a bit harsh but it is nevertheless true. If it weren't, there wouldn't be so much pain and panic at the thought of retirement. In fact, athletes remind me of playboys. Neither knows when to call it quits. And fate does tend to play cruel tricks by sending confusing signals. A lucky punch or a perfectly played set can mislead the ageing jock into thinking the old magic is still there. So it is up to the manager or coach or even the hack to tell him it is only an optical illusion. Playboys, unfortunately, do not enjoy such luxuries. There is no one to tell us when our time is up. An exceptional party, a sudden unexpected conquest, even a particularly enjoyable stay at some resort can fool one into staying on the merry-go-round for one more season. The results are always catastrophic.

Why am I having morbid thoughts just as spring is in the air? Well, for one thing I want to compete in karate again and I know that being 47 is not the perfect age for it. I also want to give tennis a try, but there I haven't got a chance. It will have to be in 45s and overs. And the thought of women doesn't help either. There are no age limits where the fair sex is concerned, so I have to compete with people half my age on an equal footing. I think the law should be changed. Mr Leon Brittan, having already been extremely kind to me once, could be even kinder by passing the fairest law of all: that older men should be given a handicap when competing for a younger lady.

· Soapbox ·

New York · I was limping up Park Avenue after some mayhem at the karate dojo when I noticed a good-looking blonde girl staring at me in that particularly shifty-eyed manner people assume when unsure whether or not they should say hello. Upon closer inspection it turned out to be Miss Catherine Oxenberg, the latest British (Yugoslav-American really) import gracing *Dynasty*, the soap opera that is doing for the rich in America what the alleged remark of Marie-Antoinette concerning cake did for the house of Louis Capet. When she finally did say hello, she was friendly although quite catty. But I was ready. 'Not to worry,' I said, 'I've got Pentonville to be ashamed of, but you've got *Dynasty*.' In all fairness, Catherine wasn't trying to be rude. Far from it. She has simply lived in New York too long, and oneupmanship in the Big Apple is what name-dropping is in Hollywood. Second nature.

Speaking of *Dynasty* and *Dallas*, I wonder who are the role models used by scriptwriters who turn out such trash every week. Although my recent neighbours were embezzlers, thieves, drug-pushers and thugs, most of them seem to be the moral superiors of the ghastly soap opera characters. (Having just read that Candy Spelling, the wife of the producer of *Dynasty*, flies the entire Dior collection over in a private aeroplane in order to view it and choose, I am beginning to get a good idea whom the characters are based on.)

And although it is only a soap opera it does manage to get its message across: that people who create the wealth in America are avaricious and dishonest and never to be trusted. Who needs *Pravda* when we have the Shylocks of Hollywood giving us the word? Well, perhaps I'm over-reacting, but in a country where there are more libraries stocking videos than there are libraries containing what libraries normally contain, I fear that *Dynasty*'s ghastly image of America might be getting across, and soon the Carringtons will be far better known than the Karamazovs. Worse, the upwardly mobile young in New York are starting to talk and act like those idiots on the television screen, which makes my life so much more difficult. Let me explain.

One thing I promised myself while languishing in Pentonville last winter was never again to get caught up in the kind of New York merry-go-round I was trapped in before my bust. The nightly rounds of chic restaurants and louche nightclubs, the staying-up all night in the company of people one would avoid even while in prison, the clocking-in at parties where there were more persons in the lavatories than on the dance floor, all those horror nights were to be a thing of the past.

My plan was simply not to go nightclubbing. Lunch and dinner and *c'est tout*. Three weeks in New York, however, and I see it is not enough. Although I have avoided the riff-raff of the louche nightclubs, I have not managed to avoid the *Dynasty*-based riff-raff that hang out in chic restaurants. The kind that refer to tables as power table number one, or two, or three. The type that count agents like Swifty Lazar and Morton Janklow as their friends (if you think Lazar is bad news, you should meet Janklow) and try to behave *à la* Joan Collins and J. R. Ewing. If you think I'm exaggerating, pay a visit to Le Cirque or Mortimer's during lunch, and the newest chic pizzeria called *Primadonna* for dinner. First of all, the women all look the same, with tough jaws, layered hairstyles, and dresses that cost as much if not more than a B-52. Their only conversation is which status symbol costs how much. The men are even worse. They wear their power look, and talk about success. It is enough to drive one back to Pentonville, or worse, to louche nightclubs.

Needless to say, having realized what I was up against after only three days in New York, I was still not ready to stay quietly at home with – heaven forbid – a book and the wife. So I did the next best thing. I decided once again to turn intellectual and had my friend Norman Mailer to dinner, followed by Bob Tyrrell, and even Haden-Guest. Mailer arrived well in his cups and he was a delight. He wanted to know all about British prisons, gave us a long account of Mohammad Ali's life at present, and admitted that his 17-year-old son can now handle his case in the boxing ring. He also told a marvellous story about Harry K. Thaw, the man who murdered Stanford White, the great architect who was portrayed on the screen by Mailer himself in the movie *Ragtime*.

Thaw served 15 years and after being released was shown the new family house by his adoring mother. 'Oh, my God,' he screamed, 'I shot the wrong architect.' The house was the type people in *Dynasty* think has class. Fifteen years in the clink made Thaw a wise man. That is more than I can say for the *Dynasty* people and those who act like them.

· Dining with Dicky ·

As ex-Presidents of the United States go, the only one I'd cross the ocean in order to dine with is that darling of the liberals, Richard Milhous Nixon. The first time I met him was at Jonathan Aitken's house, where he addressed a Tory philosophy group I head whenever I'm out of prison. We hit it off well, so well in fact that he wrote to me while I was in Pentonville. There is something extremely touching (and rare) about an ex-President writing to one who is banged up. After all, politicians are known to be a bit like art dealers and Charles Benson, never there when you need them. So, when my friend Bob Tyrrell rang and told me I was included in an off-the-record dinner with Nixon, I left Annabel's and flew to New York, destination New Jersey, via stops at Southampton and Watermill, Long Island, for a weekend tennis tournament in which no one competing had a good word to say about Tiriac or McEnroe.

The Nixon house is in Saddle River, a very green and beautiful part of New Jersey, one hour from New York City. The house has a Japanese garden of about five acres, a swimming pool that looks like a lotus pond, a tennis court (for the children) and is furnished and covered with the kind of chintzes that Arabs might find vulgar but we English fought the second world war in order to preserve. It is a sprawling house, on one storey, as Mrs Nixon is not in the best of health and cannot climb stairs. The colours are soft browns and yellows, with modern and old mixed up, everything orderly yet cosy. The famous man waited just inside the glass door and came out to greet us as we drove up.

If one wasn't prejudiced against Richard Nixon – which few people are not thanks to the two greatest novelists since Tolstoy (Woodward has since gone on to greater triumphs, with a hatchet job on the dead Belushi, while Bernstein concentrated on Margaret Jay) – it would be easy to see why the press distrust him. He simply is not good at all at small-talk. And as everyone knows, it's charm, small-talk and badinage with the reporters, *à la* JFK, that the American media consider important. Reagan is a natural at it, Nixon is not, never was. What he is is brilliant. There is no other word for him. He knows it all, has seen it all, has met everyone, has had his finger on the button longer than anyone. I only wish Reagan, Carter and Ford had abducted him, stuck him in a large wing of the State Department, fired nine tenths of the decision makers, let him run our foreign policy and this would be a far better world to live in.

As the meeting was off the record I cannot write about the important things, like Star Wars, and our chances of having an all-out nuclear exchange. Of course, Richard Nixon must know that anything said in the presence of eight journalists has as much of a chance of remaining off the record as, say, Harold Pinter is likely to choose places like Vietnam, Afghanistan, Poland, Bulgaria, Cuba and Nicaragua before he chooses to go to Turkey and proclaim that writers over there are being picked on. (Not to mention the Soviet Union, eh Harold?)

We first talked for about 45 minutes, then went into the yellow Chinese room for drinks and canapés, then into dinner. That consisted of excellent filet-mignon, vegetables, cheese and a very good chocolate mousse. The wine was Château Latour '66, 'a good year for wines, a bad one for politics,' according to our host. From there we went into his study where the mood became more relaxed. He even told us a few anecdotes about the great men of his time.

Curiously enough, Nixon is a dove in domestic politics. He admires Reagan and speaks to him often but is more of a centrist than R. R. But when it comes to the Soviet Union, he is more of a hawk than the cowboy. (His analysis of the hostage crisis and his opinion on what should have been done was brilliant.) He calls the Soviets nuclear coercers, not fools, nor stupid, just greedy. He thinks that when the Soviets decide to take out the Chinese nuclear capability, it will bring the Western alliance to a terrible dilemma. He knows more about the Soviet Union than all of the CIA put together. I guess that's why people who don't like to see a strong America still hate and fear him. People like those who want Reagan to resign simply because he's now a semicolon. I only hope they hold their breath till he does.

· The fatherland ·

Zante · Zante is the most southerly of the Ionian islands, north-west of the Peloponnese and the nearest point to it, a little less than ten miles away. There are 30,000 inhabitants, most of whom have no Turkish blood running in their veins, a rare phenomenon among modern Greeks. The reason for this is that the Zantiotes did not live for 400 years under Turkish rule, so they escaped the Levantine features and tastes of their fellow Neo-Hellenes. The island is the birthplace of Greece's most important poets, Solomos and Kalvos being two examples, as well as Italy's greatest bard, Hugo Foscolo. More important than that, however, is the fact that Taki's father and provider was born there 77 years ago.

Zante's history would make a soap opera to end all soap operas. Every pirate west of Bora Bora seems to have passed through and taken a shot at the place, and many have left their influence on the island, even Cervantes. The Spanish writer lost his leg off the western coast while serving as a seaman on a galleon that was attacked by pirates. The Venetians and the English were the two powers that stayed the longest, although the Brits have left very little behind to remind one of them, with the exception of recalcitrant civil servants and a funny game called *kriket* that no one plays any more due to the fact that England is run by a woman.

What I used to love about Zante was the way people dressed – men in white suits, ladies with parasols – and the way the townsfolk used to promenade up and down the main square at sunset. In the house of Dionyssis Romas, a poet and friend who is now dead, I used to look at portraits of his family and mine, people whom the *Guardian* would label exploiters, and an honest man, nobles. The costumes were made of silk. The men wore wigs and were clean-shaven. The ladies wore long trains and black veils. In 1821 many of those people in the family portraits became members of the *Filiki Eteria*, or Society of Friends, people who gave large amounts of money to free Greece from the Ottoman yoke. At times, when my bar bill at Annabel's begins to resemble the Soviet investment in the European anti-nuclear movement, I wonder whether it was worth it;

when I'm in Greece, and hear the shrill anti-Western rhetoric of the clowns that run this place, I become convinced it was not. But when in Zante I change my mind. The people have not as yet become completely tourist-minded, though the signs are there.

The whole town of Zakynthos was flattened by the disastrous earthquakes and the subsequent fires of 1953. Almost every great and noble house of the Venetian period fell. The new town began in the old pattern but then the greedy types took over as they always do. The houses now resemble the Greek style, the modern one, which makes Zante a pretty ugly place to be in.

Three quarters of Zante is covered by low mountains, and the island is green, full of pines, orchards, vineyards and olive trees. My papa's lands are mostly inland, although we do own a large beach called Alexandra's on which we plan to build yet another modern horror in order to make enough money to support our lifestyle. This will be the first Taki-owned land to go commercial in over 200 years, something I'm hardly proud of but last time I tried to pay in a nightclub with an olive tree it was not appreciated. And in view of what I saw taking place last Sunday evening in the main square, Solomos Place, frankly, my dear, I don't give a damn any more.

There I was, waiting to sail off into the night with daddy's stinkpot, when I became aware of some activity in the square. I wandered off to see what all the noise was about. It was a communist youth rally, a concert of sorts, one that gave away free books by Lenin, and free books by any writer who believes America to be the most oppressive and fascist state in the world. There was also a picture of Moscow on the screen and underneath it, 'Moscow, peace capital of the world'. I went back to the boat and told my father that I wouldn't give a damn even if he built a Hilton-like hotel on our beach. His eyes lit up. It seems there are ways communism can make someone happy.

· Paris revisited ·

Papa Hemingway knew a thing or two when he wrote: 'Paris is like a mistress who does not grow old and always has other lovers.' Unlike people who live in the present, Hemingway's emotions existed in the past, and Paris was a place that I suspect gave him more pain than pleasure towards the end. It is not hard to understand why, either. Paris never really changes, the smells are the same, the taxi drivers are the same, the Parisians are the same. Nostalgia is the city's cheapest commodity.

A cynic might ask, nostalgia for what? Again, an easy question to answer. Primarily nostalgia for one's youth. Or in my case, the time when I thought of nothing other than chasing girls, going to nightclubs, and riding an Argentine off in front of the clubhouse of the Polo Club in the Bois. In Papa's case Paris meant the place where it all began, where the trip really started, and as everyone knows, the voyage is what counts, not the arrival.

As I said, the trouble with Paris is that nothing changes. Go down the rue de Bac, turn left on the rue de Lille, and you see the tiny *pension* that once served as your favourite *cinq à sept* rendezvous during the late Fifties. Or walk up the rue François Ier, and in the corner of the rue Pierre Charon there is La Belle Ferronnière, the bistro where the *Paris Match* boys used to hang out, as well as all sorts of ladies of the night. One of the waiters asks you why you've stayed away for so long, which doesn't make it any easier. Best of all, drive on up the boulevard Montparnasse and dine at the Closerie des Lilas with Parisian friends who speak of nothing except the beauty of women, a typical French habit that is full of gentility and fun. At the Closerie the ghosts are real. The piano player plays tunes you heard almost 30 years ago, and you recognize a couple of faces from way back then.

After the hell of Athens Paris seems even more beautiful. This time I chose to stay at a small hotel on the Right Bank in order to be close to where my children are staying. My room is huge, with a large fireplace and windows that start at the floor and rise almost to 14 feet. Every morning I look out over the grey slate Parisian roofs

and listen to the sounds of the city waking up. As I'm with the wife and children I am drinking very little and not night-clubbing at all. *Ergo* I'm up at the time I used to go to bed when I lived here. The effect is one and the same. There is nothing like Paris at daybreak.

The only changes I've noticed in Paris are that there are now more Arabs. And more places in which they keep the money they have ripped off us since 1973. Even Merrill Lynch, which used to be in front of the Travellers Club near Le Rond Point, has gone oily. It is now the Bank of Dubai. As far as buildings are concerned, the French are light years ahead of the rest of Europe. There is a blot on the Left Bank where the Tour Montparnasse stands like an undulating finger (middle finger) to good taste, and there is Le Baubourg. Otherwise the Palumbos of this world have failed in Paris. They've ruined the vista through the Arc, but that is about all. The French know how to preserve their heritage.

And they know how to commemorate French heroes. All last week I wandered around Paris seeing some old friends, but mostly showing Paris to my four-year-old boy, and nine-year-old daughter. Our favourite visit was to Les Invalides. My boy was open-mouthed when he saw the tomb of the great Napoleon (especially when I let it slip that we have the same birthday). We also saw the tomb of Marshal Duroc, the man who first approached Maria Walewska *de la part de l'Empéreur*, and who died by taking a direct hit while galloping next to Bonaparte. When my son saw a first world war taxi (there to commemorate the part taxis played in saving Paris in 1917) he asked me, 'Is that Napoleon's taxi, Papa?'

Well, it might be hard for young children to understand about glory and heroic deeds, but the message can be got across. All one has to do is to take one's children to Les Invalides, rather than the movies. And maybe my visit there is the best thing I've done so far for my daughter. It might keep her from falling for such un-Invalides-like people as Warren Beatty or Keith Richards one day. Let's hope so.

· Setting sights ·

I think it's time for me to move on. The great American climber invasion has begun, and there is no room on these isles for both Taki and those in search of dukes and ducks. Only last week I was dining at Annabel's when, from the table next to mine, this terrific bore explained in a very loud voice how much he spent every year shooting in England. After a while I couldn't stand it any more, and just before the main course I asked Louis to move me. Needless to say, my new location was no better. Except that the second bore was a nicer type of American, more innocent and less pretentious. He kept repeating the fact that he was off 'to hunt grouse', and I longed to ask him whether he would wear a purple coat.

Now please don't get me wrong. There is no one more pro-American than the poor little Greek jailbird, but I draw the line where rich American social climbers are concerned. I also know that social climbing is not a recent phenomenon, but has been around as long as time immemorial. (In fact, the very first Ancient Greek social climber was one Menelaus, who married into the Taki family, a certain Helen Taki, if memory serves me right.) What bothers me is that come autumn the *nouveaus* seem to get into a frenzy, especially American ones from the East Coast. What they do is land over here *en masse*, buy out all the Purdeys and tweeds Britain can produce, pay through the nose (no pun intended) to people who own shoots, and bore the pants off innocent bystanders like me whenever I have the bad luck to be in their vicinity while they recount tall tales about shooting with earls, marquesses and dukes.

Once upon a time, hearing such nonsense was fun. Especially when their lock-jawed wives would complain about the vulgarity of peers who talked openly about their running cocks and being pricked. My favourite story was of the Greek shipowner who decimated a group of newly rich record-company executives by shooting across the line of guns. While they lay writhing in their brand new tweeds and cursing the Greek, as well as their stretch limo chauffeurs for not warning them the man couldn't see, the predictable happened. One of the social-climbing wives ran hysterically into a nearby village and summoned the fuzz. When the host explained to the cops that the offender was a guest and that he was the finest shot in Greece, the officer was not impressed. 'No wonder,' muttered the copper, 'the way he shoots he must be the only one left.'

This is not to say that the indigenous social climbers are hibernating, however. Come the hunting season (and I don't mean grouse) the local mountaineers are out in force. Take, for example, my good friend Sebastian Taylor. He is probably the most accomplished and sophisticated social mountaineer there is. For years he climbed on the backs of peers' daughters, or wives, but now that he's getting on, past 30, he's decided to climb on a horse. 'I just need that blue and boff,' (*sic*) he told me last time I saw him, 'and I'll never have a problem again.' He was referring to the Beaufort hunt, needless to mention, and the next thing I knew he got himself invited to Badminton, which in turn caused Bounder Basualdo to have a nervous breakdown.

Speaking of Badminton and the Beauforts, I spent my last English weekend there, probably the only non-royal weekend in that wonderful house. (Taylor got himself invited to one with royals, even if it was only with Princess Michael.) The topic of the conversation was Bounder Basualdo, and how he was up at 4 a.m. in order to be ready to go cubbing with the Duke. When I asked the bounder how come he was feeling so energetic suddenly, he said to me: 'I love his Grace the Duke of Beaufort more than I love even Christina Onassis!!!!'

And no social-climbing story would be complete without a mention of the ingenious manner that Nigel Politzer, known among us jailbirds as 'the rat', discovered to keep himself with people born above his station. He simply volunteered to become the manager of the Business Connection – proving himself an immediate success in promoting them – and he's now seen seven days a week discussing business with his clients, people like Teresa Manners, John Somerset, Michael Cecil, Harry Worcester *et al.*

· Cast of villains ·

New York · All that training and worrying went to waste. A bureaucratic hitch kept me out of Japan and the world shotokan karate championship. Worse, it marooned me in New York in the middle of a hurricane and among the motliest group of strutting political peacocks this side of Beirut. Yes, I do mean the so-called statesmen who at this very moment are wining and dining themselves like the brothers Karamazov at the New York taxpayer's expense. This is the United Nations' 40th anniversary and most of the world's oppressors are here, or on their way to these shores, in order to address the most ridiculous body since that of Quasimodo. Needless to say, their presence here needs the kind of protection it warrants back home, which means whole blocks sealed off, sharp-shooters on every roof, hundreds of policemen on overtime – the works. Protection increases in direct proportion to the number of the leader's fellow nationals residing here – i.e. Castro will need it constantly because there are a lot of Cubans here, as will Jaruzelski of Poland. Even more ironic is the fact that it is the countries that call themselves democratic and socialist which need the most guards.

The city of New York is picking up the bill for the extravaganza, which means that I, and the rest of the suckers living here, will be paying for it. Which leads me to believe that there is something terribly wrong with American democracy in general, and the kind practised by New York in particular. I am convinced that if there was a vote on whether the UN should be allowed to remain here, the only pro votes would be cast by those free-loaders posted here as members of the most bloated body since that of King Farouk.

While the hurricane threatened, people like Governor Cuomo (a man with Peter-Hall-like appetite where others' money is concerned) constantly went on television assuring the people that they and their honoured guests would be given adequate protection from the elements. Wrath of God would have been closer to the truth. And it was altogether fitting that following the first speaker God let loose with the kind of protest not seen in these parts since 1938. Yes, it was the man who serves the heroes of Afghanistan, Prague, Budapest, the Berlin Wall, Estonia, Latvia, Lithuania and the Ukraine who spoke first, soon followed by the man who brought down Solidarity, smashed the heads of working men and imprisoned Lech Walesa.

What a cast of villains. Castro and the mad Gaddafi are both expected, and both will be given the platform of the UN, the ear of the world, and even credence by some, while they spread their message of mayhem and mutual hatred of those who pick up the bill. And speaking of bills, Castro's latest antic is a campaign of personal diplomacy to get Latin-American nations to knock the $361 billion they owe to US banks. (It serves people like David Rockefeller right for shelling out to clowns like the Brazilians, but it is small fry like Taki whose loans are called in first when the big ones default.)

Even funnier than the speeches and posturing of the Castros of this world, are the shenanigans of some that serve them. For example: Mexico's ambassador to the UN, Porfirio Munoz-Ledo, pulled a gun on a motorist and broke the window of his car because the taxpayer had parked 18 inches inside his 'personal diplomatic parking space'. No charges were filed. North Korea's third secretary, O Nam Chol, sexually molested a New York woman and then took sanctuary in his mission for a year. He then fled the country.

The list is long. I could go on and on but I won't. What I will do is try and protest by not paying city tax this year, which means not buying anything in the city. How will I manage it? Easy. I am moving to Southampton, Long Island, for the duration of my stay here. Not only am I unable to see the UN from there, but I cannot smell it either.

· Drug deals ·

New York · I turned on the television last Friday evening in order to watch the news and I got a bit of a shock. There was Anthony Haden-Guest giving a press conference of sorts, in my flat in Knightsbridge, a press conference to all three major American networks. As soon as I got over the shock I rang my flat in London. Needless to say, it was busy, and stayed busy until I went to bed cursing the day I had the bad luck to run into Haden-Guest 15 years ago – which, incidentally, is just about the time I began to become seriously poor. Worse was to come the next morning. That is when I read in the *New York Post* that the writer Haden-Guest had given a two-hour interview to the *Post* detailing his kidnapping and heroic escape from his Lebanese captors. Immediately I rang a friend who works on Rupert Murdoch's organ and asked him to make inquiries whether Anthony had rung the *Post* or vice versa.

To my horror, my contact reported it was the former. That is when I went into a deep depression, one which has as yet to lift, cursing the day those murdering Lebanese gangsters decided to take it easy for once. When I finally got through to the uninvited guest a strange voice answered but immediately identified himself as a policeman. Like all cops he began by asking me questions like who was I and what was my business, etc. So I identified myself and told him I was asking the questions this time. 'Oh, well then,' he answered, 'there's this gentleman 'ere, who claims to live 'ere, but was sleeping outside on the pavement when we found 'im this morning. 'E also claims 'e 'asn't his keys on 'im. So we 'ad to 'elp 'im break in.'

Then Haden-Guest came on the line and told me not to worry, that he was all right, safe, and now on his way to New York to tell all for a large fee. 'Can we have dinner tonight?' was the last thing he asked me.

It is at times such as these that one has to show character, and I did. I even invited him to dinner and heard the most extraordinary tale since Clifford Irving interviewed Howard Hughes. Here it is in a nutshell: it was just about one year ago that a convicted drug-dealer named Steven Donahue (this is one of many names) contacted

Haden-Guest and asked him to become his Boswell. Donahue had been caught by the Drug Enforcement Agency and in turn had decided to work with them in Lebanon. Donahue had read Anthony's book about the murder of the lover of a beautiful model by her ex-lover, and found Haden-Guest to be just the right man to write well about bad things happening to bad people. Haden-Guest, who is the hungriest man born north of Khashoggi's birthplace, accepted with alacrity. While I whiled away my days in Pentonville, those two were prancing around Beirut, digging up information, but also having a hell of a time, according to the permanent Guest.

The Christian gunmen and drug-dealers who were their hosts liked Anthony. Every day he passed out and, while terrific gun fights would have everyone ducking for cover, Anthony would walk about undisturbed by the noise and danger looking for free drinks, which he was given non-stop by his 'captors', in order to show their young militiamen what courage is all about. In the meantime the group of drug-dealers found out that Donahue was working for the DEA and decided to make money out of it instead of adding another two corpses to Beirut's list. They played Donahue along and got the DEA to pay a large sum for some pretty bad pot. Then they told Anthony he could leave, but kept Donahue behind.

When Anthony returned in order to gather more material, another group of Arab drug-runners decided they wanted part of the DEA money too, and abducted the two from their abductors. They, too, decided to let Anthony go after a couple of weeks as their supplies of food and drink quickly ran out, and none of them had the heart to let Anthony go hungry or thirsty. Now Anthony is back here, has all the material he needs, the Arabs have screwed the DEA, Donahue is under arrest in Beirut, and I'm out of pocket for at least 1,000 quid. Not to mention the damage to my flat by a large group of dirty electronic hacks. But I have learned one thing that few know as of now. The whole bloody business in Lebanon has to do with drugs and absolutely, positively nothing else. Least of all politics.

· Protection racket ·

New York · My first marriage got off on the wrong foot partly because of Peter Lawford, the British-born actor now resting in place unknown. (I would bet below.) Lawford was a heavy drinker, and used to get awfully nasty when intoxicated. One of his favourite tricks was to tell my then extremely pretty young bride what a terrible shit I was, and how I chased ugly women behind her back. Now, there is nothing that will get a pretty girl on her high horse quicker than the realization that her man chases ugly women. Pursuing beauty makes the wife competitive, while the pursuit of an ugly woman makes the wife seek revenge.

Somehow Lawford knew this and played it to the hilt. Christina too. In no time I found myself in the doghouse because of Lawford's indiscretions, and confronted him with them. (We shared a flat at the Sherry Netherland Hotel at the time.) Lawford became abusive and almost violent, and his agent had to separate us. I couldn't well move out and leave my bride behind, so I stayed. Which is the one thing Peter did not want. There were still enough Kennedys and their groupies dropping in on him, and Taki was in the way. So the wife and I moved out, and it was the last I ever saw of him. That was 1965. Twenty years later he's once again in the news over here – and I gather over there, also – and it all has to do with the Kennedys, Marilyn Monroe, and some murky details concerning her death.

Needless to say, if any other family had been involved with Marilyn Monroe, the Nixons, say, we would never have had Watergate. In fact, I am ready to bet my last drachma that Richard Nixon would have been disqualified from running for dog-catcher, let alone the Presidency of the United States. But as we all know the Kennedys are not the Nixons. They enjoy privileges that ordinary mortals cannot aspire to – like the protection of the press, the intelligentsia, and now it seems even the television networks; well, the president of ABC News, Roone Arledge, to be exact. Arledge is known for his venturesome television journalism, as he is known for his close friendship with the Kennedys. He has just cancelled a programme that insiders say proved almost beyond reasonable doubt that Bobby

Kennedy was in Los Angeles the night MM died, and furthermore that he had a lot to do with her death. The programme also includes on-air interviews with people who say they bugged Marilyn's house in order to trap Kennedy, and they did it on the orders of Jimmy Hoffa, the gangster leader of the Teamsters Union that Bobby had sworn to send to jail.

And there is more. Marilyn was known as an inveterate scribbler, someone who kept diaries of everything and everybody she came into contact with. Nothing was found after her death. Worse, there is a policeman who swears that Kennedy and his friends tried to shut up La Monroe by offering her pills and other sedatives that fateful night. Finally, there are hints that Bobby and JFK had contact with Sam Giancanna, a well-known Mafia leader. For me the hints are good enough. I knew Sam Giancanna as Sam Moody, had been introduced to him by Peter Lawford, and had heard the actor and the mobster talk fondly of the Kennedys and reminisce about past shenanigans with the 'first' family. Shenanigans, I may add, that cannot be repeated in a glossy weekly like the *Spectator*.

But to get back to Arledge. An ABC newsman described his (Arledge's) refusal to run the programme as unfortunate: 'He's in bed with the Kennedys,' was the way he put it. Little did the newsman know how close to the truth he was. The hack forgot to mention that Jeff Ruhe, an Arledge top assistant, is married to Courtney Kennedy, the fifth of Bobby's 11 children, and David Burke, vice-president of ABC News, is a former aide to the senator from Massachusetts.

What is it about the Kennedys that makes them forbidden ground for television, press, and even police investigation? As far as I'm concerned, it is fear of reprisals. They are still enormously powerful and well connected, and people who have crossed them have not exactly prospered. I have no details, but will recount only a rather sordid story that involved a Kennedy member. A girl I knew was beaten up badly enough to have to stay in bed for two weeks. She had apparently been out with this character, shared his drugs but refused to share his bed. He went berserk and she went to hospital. When I saw her I begged her to give me an affidavit so I could write the story. She paled when she heard me. 'They'll kill you and me,' was the only thing she said when she realized what I was after. The girl has since returned to England. And I will let you draw your own conclusions.

· Gentlemen-at-arms ·

New York · I witnessed a terrible fight last week, one that left me longing for the days when gentlemen settled their differences in a chivalrous way, with lances, swords, pistols, even whips. I was with my friend Chuck Pfeiffer, a very tough ex-Green Beret captain who won the Silver Star in Vietnam, and we were dining in one of the trendiest restaurants down in Greenwich Village. The fight started suddenly, and to our amazement involved three men, all perfectly respectable and seemingly well-educated. But it was vicious and two people got badly hurt. Chuck stopped it while I covered his back, as he yelled for me to do. The restaurant owner sent over a bottle of champagne to thank us but I was no longer in the mood. I guess I'm getting old and no longer enjoy fights.

Long ago, it could never have happened. One weapon that was rarely used by angry or insulted folk was the human fist. Satisfaction was usually had after a little bloodletting, although at times things did tend to get out of hand – no pun intended – and severe injury occurred. Duelling separated the patricians from the plebeians and also ensured a certain decorum and standard of behaviour among the upper classes, an unheard of phenomenon among today's moneyed classes.

Duelling might seem a senseless custom today, but it did manage to keep society extremely polite. A few hasty words might mean a challenge, and more often than not, one or both of the combatants had reason to regret his loss of temper. Although it was illegal to fight duels, the law was seldom enforced. Usually there was a trial only after one of the duellists had been killed. The survivor, generally, was charged with manslaughter and given a very light sentence. The unwritten rule was that if one happened to kill one's adversary, especially if the victor had issued the challenge, he would exile himself for a decent interval. After that, everything would return to normal.

Sometimes the dying loser would not only forgive his adversary with his last breath but might even accept the blame. Such was the case in a famous duel between Colonel Richard Thornhill and Sir Cholmley Dering, which took place in 1711 and resulted in the latter's death. Thornhill had insisted on the duel after Sir Cholmley had stepped on his foot after a long bout of drinking. As Sir Cholmley lay dying he said that the duel was of his own seeking. Thornhill never served a day.

His dying gesture was recognized as typical gentlemanly behaviour. Some of the most famous duels have been fought over differ-

ences of opinion that would be barely noticed in today's permissive and certainly dishonourable times, when vanity is more important than pride. I will not dwell on the famous duels that have been fought in the past. They are well-known and I haven't the space. I will, however, mention a few that have taken place since the second world war. The best-known was fought by two men I knew. It was an artistic duel in more ways than one. It took place in Paris in 1958, between the Marquis de Cuevas, of ballet fame, and Serge Lifar, the Russian-born choreographer. Cuevas was 72 at the time and Lifar 53. Lifar had flung his scented handkerchief at Cuevas during the intermission at the Black and White ballet. They met at an estate 50 miles from Paris, and after a lot of weaving and bobbing, Cuevas pricked Lifar in the arm. Then Cuevas burst into tears and collapsed. The bleeding Lifar consoled him. They embraced and it was all over.

There have been at least seven duels at Oxford and Cambridge since the war, employing sabres, rapiers, umbrellas, even champagne corks. The most unusual was fought by – who else – Anthony Haden-Guest. He was challenged by a Greek schoolmate while at Gordonstoun. The Greek insisted on javelins at 50 paces, however. Both missed, although Anthony's javelin was embedded in a nearby plane tree.

Duelling would work wonders if it came back today. At the very least, it would restore a touch of dignity to late-night proceedings in Manhattan bars and allow one to finish a meal in peace. Only two days after Pfeiffer and I had witnessed that bad brawl downtown, we saw another one, this time in a place that was far more chic. A man lost his temper with two gays who were making fun of him and decided to slap one of them. He missed and hit a girl who was with them. The two gays scratched him and called him names. Pfeiffer and I let that one go on.

· Café royal ·

New York · I often wrote about Mortimer's, the brick-lined, dark-panelled restaurant that looks like the inside of a fireplace and is known as the 'in' place of the trendies, during the days when I reported on the high life from the front lines – i.e. when I used to go out every single night and write about it. Now that I've become a sort of homebody, I only go to Mortimer's for lunch (well, dinner only twice a week) and as everyone knows, the only good thing that ever happens during lunch is if it is in preparation for a *cinq à sept* assignation. Mortimer's is ten years old this year, as, incidentally, is my little daughter. Lolly was just born when a friend of mine took me to the opening of Mortimer's. The place was a mess, I thought, and I was ready to wager my little girl's dowry that it wouldn't last out the year. Thank God I had no takers.

Not only did the place survive, it has become an institution of sorts. Every biggie and *soi disant* big cheese in the Big Apple is a regular there, which is probably the only thing I don't like about the place. Things I do like are the proprietor, the people who serve on the tables, the preppies who frequent it, the drinks, the location (four blocks from *chez* Taki) and the food. In that order. What I don't like, as I just mentioned, are some of the social climbers and stuffed mummies that *Women's Wear* takes seriously but who one day will be assigned by history to the rubbish bin that's marked Trivial with a capital T. You know the kind, the type who do social work among the rich, and consider Jerry Zipkin to be a wit on a par with Oscar Wilde.

But I guess it takes all kinds to make a place work, and Mortimer's works. What a cast it assembles each and every day. There is Jackie K. O., always in dark glasses in case someone fails to recognize her; and Kenneth J. Lane, the designer of false jewels, which are really very beautiful, but not as beautiful as the false British accent and aristocratic aplomb Kenny has perfected over the years. There is also Louis Basualdo, looking for any heiress whose father might not have heard of him, the *de rigueur* British contingent of swells looking for someone to freeload off. The last Englishman to pick up a tab was Claus von Bülow. And ladies like Jane Wrightman, who looks down her nose at people, speaks without opening her mouth and is only seen in the company of the very rich and famous, but who, despite all this, has as yet been unable to obscure her rather humble origins.

Needless to say, there are nice people who go there too, but I shall not mention them because nice people don't like to be mentioned. Someone I will mention is the man who tried to take over Mortimer's in a manner that would be unacceptable even in Beirut. That was Stefanos, a countryman of mine (although no relation). Glenn Bernbaum, the owner of Mortimer's, and a hell of a nice man as well as a gent, picked the Greek up somewhere in the Aegean and brought him back to New York. Once ensconced in the city, Stefanos revealed the fact that he had a wife and children, and Glenn – ever the gentleman – paid for their trip over. That is when Stefanos got greedy. Glenn had left the place to him, and Stefanos, like many Greeks, insisted on instant gratification. He hired two hoods to bump Glenn off. But like many Greeks he got it wrong. The two hoods turned out to be FBI men, and instead of inheriting the *numero uno* watering hole in New York, Stefanos inherited a place in the hole, *c'est tout*. Glenn did not press charges, however, and the greasy Greek was simply deported as an undesirable.

The reason I bring up this old story is because I have decided to do my utmost to be adopted by Glenn in order that some day I can play Rick, and not in a hole like Casablanca either. When I first proposed it to Bernbaum he thought I was joking, but after I began to call him Baba – a Greek way of saying Daddy – the idea sounded less and less ludicrous. I now sign my cheques 'Stefanos' and I've even stopped insulting the *Women's Wear* crowd in order to make myself popular. The first thing I will do if I ever inherit the place is give a dinner for the staff and make some of the ladies I mentioned serve them. But Zipkin will have to stay in the kitchen.

1986

· Paradise isle ·

St Barthelemy · Imagine what the Caribbean was 25 years ago, before the 3,000-mile-long necklace of islands stretching from the Bahamas to South America became as popular as Cannes and Monte Carlo, and you'll have a pretty good idea what St Bart's is like. Picture empty beaches, a leisurely rhythm of life, cacti of various shapes, emerald-green or turquoise-coloured water, a lush and mountainous interior and a few tourists with nothing much to do except swim, sunbathe, windsurf, snorkel and drink rum punches, and you'll get the perfect picture of St Bart's. More important, you'll understand why it's the only island to visit during a time of year everyone – including the muggers of the South Bronx – seems to be holidaying down here.

St Barthelemy is a small island, inhabited by 2,500 whites, and it lies south-east of St Maarten, in the part of the Caribbean known as the Lesser Antilles. It is French territory, without high-risers, no glass-and-concrete ranks, and without a conspicuously Guccied and Cartiered crowd. In the one week I spent here I counted two stinkpots among the yachts that anchored around the island. Needless to say, one was American-owned, the other British. Just as needless to mention is the fact that the owners of both those gigantic stinkpots turned out to be the types of fellow Armand Hammer, or perhaps George Weidenfeld, would feel at home with, which meant that along with the cooling breezes, the beautiful topless girls, and the excellent rum drinks, my group also had two figures of fun adding to our pleasurable stay.

Happily, there were countless sailing boats, including the one I was on, a 71-foot ketch called *Miss Two*, chartered by us from a friend of mine at a price that was hardly friendly but certainly reasonable. My friend Chuck (not von Bülow) Pfeiffer, two other rugged types, and a few girls, plus the excellent crew, made up what by the end of the week was known as the noisiest boat to hit St Bart's since that of Jean Lafitte, the infamous pirate who made his home in St Bart's while preying on defenceless ships.

And speaking of Jean Lafitte, here is a brief history of the island.

It seems that everyone on the island is descended from the infamous pirate, as he fathered more children than a Kikuyu chief, and bedded down more women than Darryl Zanuck while head of 20th Century Fox. And it certainly looks as if the legend is true. Never have I seen a more look-alike people. Everyone on the island looks exactly ... like everyone else. In fact they all look like Pinocchio, with funny long upturned noses, small foreheads, grey eyes, and mousy, straw-coloured hair. They speak a patois French, and are extremely friendly. St Bart's was discovered by Columbus, and its population of blood-thirsty Caribbean Indians was finally overcome by Norman seamen. In 1784 Louis XVI exchanged the island with the King of Sweden, Gustav III, for ... the use of a warehouse in the port of Gothenburg. In 1877, Sweden sold it back to France for less money than it took Onassis to buy his Ionian isle. The descendants of Jean Lafitte are mostly all white, with a mixture of Breton, Norman and Swedish blood and a character that defies description. They are childlike, a bit melancholy, hard-working, and very clean. After St Bart's, the other islands felt like Pentonville, at least to me.

The town is made up of old colonial stucco green houses, with red tile roofs, and there are quaint restaurants and bars along the narrow streets. The gendarmerie and the port captain are among those who are not inbred, and who are from mainland France. I made friends with the port captain, an old salt who had fought alongside *La Légion* in Indo-China. Although his speciality was to go out every day and scream at English boats anchored in places reserved for others, he and my group became instant friends when he discovered that Chuck (not von Bülow) Pfeiffer and I had been to Vietnam. In fact, on New Year's Eve he kept a club open after hours and opened bottle after bottle of champagne toasting *La Légion*, us, and swearing at the cowards who let down the brave men who fought there. It was *Honorary Consul* and *Under the Volcano* stuff, but noisier and with a French twist, one that I preferred.

We spent our time swimming (over a mile a day) and running on the beach, and twice we organized races with other boats round the island. With Taki at the helm, we even managed to rip a jib just as I thought my brilliant manoeuvre upwind would humiliate the Yankee boat we were racing. The skipper didn't get angry at my pressing it to such an extent, but he did point out that being competitive in St Bart's was contrary to the spirit of the place. And he was right. The last person to fight hard out there was Lafitte, and we all know what happened to him.

· Put to rights ·

New York · Well, two down and two to go to tie with Jeffrey Bernard. Marriages, that is. Last week the mother of my children and I decided to have an amicable divorce. The breakthrough came early in the week, when my own attorneys informed me that adultery applies to men also, something which I swear on the Koran I was unaware of.

So, Alexandra and I sat down with them and in no time at all agreed on an amicable separation and divorce, with me getting joint custody of our children while she retains the house and some other incidentals. Oh, yes, I almost forgot – I also get to keep my old Etonian tie, my Bullingdon Club bow tie and my White's Club ring.

Needless to say, the moment I signed on the dotted line, she and I fell into each other's arms. We then went to the flicks, and held hands throughout *Rocky XIV*. In fact, ever since, it's been like the proverbial second honeymoon. All smiles, tender glances and even lecherous shenanigans late at night. I guess Alexandra and I are not meant to be married, but to have children and live in sin, which we did for 12 years, until she had the brilliant idea of changing her name from Schoenburg into Taki.

I first met Alexandra when she was 16 years old and, being a friend of her parents, I immediately gave chase. It took me a couple of years, but it was worth it. The first sign of trouble came when I went to Israel to cover the Yom Kippur war. As everyone knows, war does funny things to people. One day I ran into a very attractive second lieutenant in the Israeli defence force, and managed to get her up to my room. No sooner were we inside than the telephone rang. It was a worried Alexandra from Paris.

While I regaled her with stories of my bravery under fire, the second lieutenant got bored and lit a cigarette with her Zippo lighter, a lighter that made a noise like a bazooka rocket upon impact, which gave the game away. The result was that a Dear John letter arrived in Tel Aviv just as I was leaving the place, and it took all of a month to get Alexandra to speak to me again.

The next year, the mother of my children-to-be decided that a visit to a shrink would cure me of my philandering. I went along with her for the laughs, as they say, because I believe in shrinks as much as I believe in Gaddafi's innocence. When we entered the shrink's office, we found her lying down on a sofa, and looking the worse for wear. I thought it was a ploy, but Alexandra, who was a close friend of hers, was worried. The shrink's first question – and last as it turned out – was, why did I feel obliged to chase women? I answered truthfully by saying that I had yet to meet a woman I found attractive that I didn't feel like making love to. (A normal response, I thought.)

But just as I said it, the shrink let out a primal scream that literally shook the windows, and collapsed further into the sofa. She then began to moan, which made me feel guilty as hell, and poor Alexandra almost hysterical with worry. It was, needless to say, the end of the session, but not for the reason you think. The poor woman was passing a kidney stone as I spoke, but I didn't find out that particular detail until years later. Which meant that for all that time I thought that my confession had actually driven an eminent psychiatrist to collapse in anguish.

Now, however, things are back to normal. Alexandra will live in Paris. I will live in London, my little girl will go to school in France, and John-Taki will enter boarding school in England as soon as he learns to spell his surname. We are once again one big happy family, and I wouldn't put it past us if the family suddenly grew larger. In the meantime, my moving to London will be a snip. Only five old Bics and three books. And my OE tie.

· A modern Penelope ·

New York · Well, here I am, about to be a bachelor once again. I don't know how American attorneys manage to do it, but when both parties are – as they say – willing, the great American divorce machine goes into action with amazingly quick results. A bachelor once again. It sounds almost perverse at my age, but I prefer it to being a widower – which my darling ex tells me I soon would have been if we had continued as before. Her last words were, 'I love you very much, but I don't want to end up like your mother.' What a thing to say about poor Mama! Here is this wonderful old lady who has stayed married to the same man for 53 years, and her daughter-in-law doesn't even hold her up as a role model. But perhaps Alexandra knows a thing or two I've kept secret all these years.

One of them is that not only has my mother put up with her husband's constant philandering for 53 years, she never even wanted to get married to him in the first place. The old man was known even then as being rather wild. My grandfather was a cruel man who divorced my grandmother and lived only on his lands in Zante with various local lassies, fathering illegitimate children left and right.

My father's brother, Harilaos, committed suicide when he was very young because he was unable to pay a debt of honour within 24 hours, as was the custom among Venetian gentlemen at the time. (Thank God that quaint old tradition is no longer. Otherwise I'd be deprived of most of my English friends.) My father left home soon after that, and went to live in Athens with a rich aunt. When he met my mother and her three sisters at an afternoon tea party, he knew immediately she was to be the one. He went on to see her father, probably the only honest politician and Chief Justice ever to bless the olive republic, and asked for her hand in marriage. Grandpapa was too kind a man to say no, so he made up an excuse about the older girl having to marry first. Which meant Daddy soon had a banker friend of his in hot pursuit of my Aunt Sophia.

Soon after, Sophia said yes, but my mother said no. Needless to say, that didn't stop the old boy. When my aunt's betrothal was announced in the newspapers, he included that of himself and my mother. Back then Athenian society was, to put it mildly, somewhat gentler than it is today. There was no room for scandal and, heaven forbid, for a denial in the gutter press.

My mother was duly married, albeit in tears, and has been the modern equivalent of Penelope ever since. She has lived quietly at home, praying for our souls and turning a dignified and blind eye to the shenanigans of Don Giovanni (albeit an ageing one) and the various divorces of her two sons. She regards her ex-daughters-in-law as her daughters and remains in touch with all of them. Alexandra was and remains her favourite, and last week when I rang her to announce the news she refused to come to the telephone. My father told me it was because she considers me to be the guilty party. I detected a hint of sanctimony in his voice, and asked him if he felt the same way. 'Certainly I do,' was his answer. And he added the proverbial insult that a man who allowed his wife to divorce him was no man.

He is probably right – and wiser than me. The one time my mother finally decided to go on board his sailing boat, she found him quietly sitting with his crew discussing matters of the sea. It was in Mykonos in 1967. When I heard about it I asked around and found out why. It seems that sometime during the Fifties, my father designed a large flag of a ball and chain which he kept along with the other ensigns on board. He also passed the word around in ports throughout the Greek isles, that if ever he flew the ball and chain ensign none of his friends and none of the tarts should come near the yacht. If they did, there would be more than hell to pay. When one of his minions advised him that my mother was on her way, he simply hoisted the ball and chain and you can guess the rest.

Well, now that I'm a bachelor I plan to order the same flag, but there are a couple of small problems. I do not plan to marry in the immediate future, and I have no money to buy back my boat which I sold last year. Otherwise I know that next time it will be for ever.

· Play it again, Meryl ·

Gstaad · In F. Scott Fitzgerald's short story *Babylon Revisited*, the hero, Charlie Wales, returns to Paris, the city of his youth, after a long hiatus. Things, however, are not the way he left them. The old gang has dispersed, and the ones that are still around are suffering from the debilitating effects of too much booze and far too much trust in the New York stock market.

For the first time in the thirty years that I've been coming to Gstaad, I feel a bit like Charlie Wales. Looking around the Palace Hotel lobby is a constant reminder that the Barbarians are not at the gates, but well inside them, and that the rape and the looting are about to begin.

Mind you, the ghosts are still there. That of Bobby Sweeny reminding us time and time again that 'It's a dice game, boys, it's purely a dice game.' Or that of Teddy Bassett, shaking his cup, moving his pipe from one side of his mouth to the other and saying, 'Well, I think I'm behind, but what the hell, I think I'll double.' Or that of Oakley Thorn, winning a game and ordering champagne for everyone within distance. The one I miss the most, of course, is the backgammon game itself, which ran for some 20-odd years, and which died prematurely when the modern-day hustlers were allowed to join in.

In a small village like Gstaad, the encroachment of the new tends to be almost painful. Worse, it serves as a constant reminder of past good times. The fact that those times were spent in the company of my wife and children doesn't help. Their presence seems to be everywhere. Even the Eagle Club has changed. All the good tables are now taken by ladies of a certain age that do not ski, but make sure they get up the mountains early enough to see that no skier lands a choice location during lunchtime ingestion.

But it has not been all sad memories and bad surprises. Far from it. Even the weather has suddenly come around. In fact, it has been perfect, and I now have a suntan so deep that a Hollywood type would give up name-dropping for a day in exchange. Just as the sun came out, the temperature dropped and the snow conditions turned excellent. I do my cross-country skiing in the morning, and downhill in the afternoon. The evenings have been mostly quiet, with the exception of one good party given by Mario Ruspoli, a man who hates the modern world even more than I do, and then some, as they say. Mario had a Thirties orchestra which played the kind of music that encourages contact between the sexes, and we danced far into the night. The guest *d'honneur* was Vittorio-Emmanuele, the pretender to the throne of Italy, and son of the last king. As some of you may have heard, Victor, as he's known among us old-timers, got into a spot of bother seven years ago. He fired a warning shot over the heads of some intruders, and killed an innocent man who was sleeping in his bunk in a boat anchored nearby. There was an investigation and Victor was jailed for a while, but nothing much ever transpired. The case, I believe, was squashed, and there are rumours that the family of the victim not only got rich overnight, but may even end up with an Italian title.

Victor and I used to be on friendly terms, but because I commented – almost favourably, mind you – on the shooting, the Savoy clan has stopped speaking to me. Well, there are worse things that can befall a skier. One that comes to mind is to have to read Victor's open letter to the Italian Communist Party asking for its help in order for him to be allowed to return to Italy. Needless to say, it is a naïve letter, almost as naïve as Corazon Aquino believing that if she lets out all the commies from prison, their buddies will lay down their arms. In fact the letter was so naïve the *Herald Tribune* chose to run it on its front page, which is where I read it.

And speaking of royalty, here is a story about the British one, a story I got straight from the horse's mouth, although I will never tell you which horse. It took place Christmas day, at Windsor Castle. The whole clan was present, including nephews and nieces. The Queen had requested to see the film *Plenty*, starring Meryl Streep. I have not seen it, but apparently there is a scene in it that takes place during Her Majesty's 1953 Coronation. While the television is showing Prince Philip and the Monarch being driven through the London crowds, Streep is making love behind a sofa. The TV is silent, and all one can hear are the moans of Ms Streep. According to my source, the Queen, the Queen Mother and Prince Philip all got up *en masse* and left the room. The only ones that stayed behind were the youngsters, and Princess Margaret, who laughed out loud, and said, 'Play it again, Sam.'

Well, if you don't hear from me again, it will not be an avalanche that's got me. It will be the royal connection.

· Redressing the balance ·

New York · When my friend Zographos and I were serving in the Greek navy some 25 to 30 years ago, we had the bad luck to be under a superior officer, Papaioannou, who hated our guts. Because of his connection with the then Prime Minister Venizelos, Zographos would obtain leave at will. No sooner would the orders for his leave arrive, however, than they would be cancelled by Papaioannou on the basis of national security, and the miserable Zographos would be given document after document to be typed and filed away.

My fate was worse. The egregious Papa would send me to the stockade on the slightest pretext. To this day neither Zog nor I have ever understood why that superior officer hated us so. Perhaps it was because Zographos had more money than the entire Greek navy, or the fact that my father used to anchor his yacht off Poros, where we were based, and have Zographos and me on board for a clandestine but civilized lunch. Or maybe it was because Zographos and I always had an Athenian hooker or two come down to Poros for the weekend, when they would let us out for two hours in the afternoon. The hookers would pose as our sweethearts and, while the rest of the suckers tried to flirt with the local girls, we would retire to the Hotel Splendide and work off our aggression towards Papaioannou.

Serving along with us – under us, rather – was a naïve peasant boy from the mountainous region of Epirus, called Petrounakos. He was extremely stupid, and almost as randy as he was dumb. He was also the toughest man on the island. Needless to say, Zographos and I befriended him and made contingency plans to use him against our tormentor. The opportunity came sooner than we expected. On the Greek national holiday, 25 March, we were all sent to Athens to prepare for the parade. It seemed that Papaioannou lived with his mother in the middle-class section of Athens, and that his mother was the only person in the world he was not beastly to.

Zographos had invited the ape-like Petrounakos to join us while in the capital. He told him that there was a super-secret *maison de passe*, where only the very rich and famous were accepted, and where the girls were all Hollywood movie stars making tax-free drachmas on the side. The ape-like Epirote growled on hearing that, and rubbed his loins. The catch, according to Zog, was to convince the madam of the house that one was indeed a client looking for some fun, and not an undercover police agent. 'No matter how much she protests and threatens to call the fuzz, just keep insisting that you want to get laid,' were the last instructions we gave him. Then we sent him off to the house of Commander Papaioannou.

I imagine everyone can guess the rest. Petrounakos's ardour had reached boiling point by the time he arrived at Mrs Papaioannou's very proper Athenian apartment, and perhaps he overdid it a bit. We know he ripped out the telephone when she dialled for the police, and a curtain or two when his search for the Hollywood girls proved fruitless. He left minutes before our tormentor arrived home for some supper with Mum.

For the next quarter of a century Papaioannou led a Javert-like search to find the culprit who had desecrated his home, but to no avail. The last I heard of him was that he had married a rich older woman and had become a socialist. Even more surprising, his mother survived the Petrounakos visit and lived to a ripe old age. The reason I hash all this up, however, has nothing to do with Greece, the navy, or even the fact that next week is our national holiday. It is that upon landing in New York two days ago, I heard about the scandal that has rocked Brown University, the trendiest place of learning this side of Pentonville. Two beautiful Brown co-eds have been accused of charging $250 for sex, after running ads in the university newspaper saying, 'Indulge yourself, experience unparalleled pleasure in the form of two Ivy League blondes.' Judging by their picture, 250 devalued dollars is a bargain. Now, if only I could find Petrounakos, somewhere in the mountains of Epirus, or on the high seas, I would make it up to him.

· Into action ·

New York · This is the time of year that New York begins to resemble one big cocktail party. The time the Weidenfelds, Gettys, Stassinopouloses and Zuckermans of this world descend upon the Big Apple as if they were F-111s zooming in on Tripoli and Benghazi. But, unlike the brave pilots who finally did something about the murders of innocent men, women, and children, the jet-setters I mentioned above – and others of their ilk – have been preparing their return in a fashion not dissimilar to that used by the fat man who took over France after the fall of Napoleon.

Most of them have been in places like Palm Beach and Beverly Hills doing social work among the rich, and putting the final touches to their tans. Others have been at fat farms, slimming down and getting in shape for the climbing season that will last until the middle of June. All of them have been on the telephone, giving their schedules to their press agents, who in turn inform the gossip columnists that rule this town the exact plans of the climbers.

In fact, I suspect that the briefings between press agents and gossip columnists match the seriousness and exactitude of those between the planners and pilots of a nightmare air raid over hostile territory. In return, some gossips tend to gush over the climbers, and present them to an unaware public in a manner first perfected by Hollywood long ago when introducing a future star of the silver screen.

And now to the wedding of the year, as the Stassinopoulos nuptials last week have been called. I shall not say a word about my fellow Greek's good luck in marrying Mr Huffington of Texas. The only thing I will comment on is the sight of Lord Weidenfeld in a Lord Fauntleroy suit, carrying the rings, his varicose veins sticking out of his silk stockings, while he wept tears of joy, all of which were recorded by the video camera that was hidden inside a Greek Orthodox priest's headgear.

Given the fact that from now on there will be more parties in New York than there are muggers, I tried to pace myself during the first hectic week. To no avail. One of the most amusing bashes I attended was for the birthday of a lady by the name of Mercedes Kellogg, whose husband is an ex-American ambassador, and as it so happens, a gentleman. The seating was arranged by drawing lots from a hat – a silk hat – and the names one drew were all historical ones. I drew Frederic Chopin, and was seated next to George Sand, who by some mistake turned out to be Jerry Zipkin. After some furious complaints on his part, a lady was put between us, and the dinner continued

uninterrupted from then on. It ended when my wife, for some strange reason I shall never understand, got up and did the dirtiest (sexiest) South American dance I have ever witnessed in a public place. Fortunately there were few guests left, but the story got out, and for once I am not the one to have embarrassed the Taki children.

In fact, I've done better than usual. The next night my friend Chuck Pfeiffer gave a party for his 45th birthday, and I gave a speech that for once was in good taste and even funny. I had asked for my wife to be seated between Norman Mailer and a good friend of mine, Eddie Ullmann, an air, rail and arms tycoon whom we refer to as Sir Basil Ullmann. But after her performance the night before, she was banished from the main table, and the designer Carolina Herrera was put in her place. I was aware that Chuck had friends from many walks of life, but that night I found out exactly how varied his friends really are. There was Hollywood, the arts, television, writers and even a poet, and most important of all, men who had served their country bravely and had been decorated for it. Although I may be gushing, I had such a good time I thought it could not possibly get any better. But it did get better early in the morning European time when I heard that American jets were finally bombing the Beast of Benghazi.

· Worlds apart ·

New York · Norman Mailer lives on a wide, quiet and tree-lined street overlooking the water, and from his terrace enjoys the beauty of the Manhattan skyline from afar. Norman's house is in Brooklyn, Columbus Heights to be exact, and I must say, although the night I went to dinner there it was raining and the humidity was rather high, it nevertheless reminded me of the good old pleasant days of the city, when people sat on their front doorsteps and talked to their neighbours, when the streets were empty of parked cars and devoid of muggers, and when the park benches were for lovers of different sexes.

Norman's dinners are legendary, and for good reason. He is, after all, considered by many the *numero uno* of American letters, and like most *numero uno*s of this town, he has a wide choice of acquaintances among the literary, political, sport, and even jet-set celebrities. But Mailer has never gone Hollywood. He still retains friends from childhood – as normal people tend to do – and among those he made on his way up. One is as likely to meet a small-time pug who never made it big in the ring, as one is to meet, say, one of the greatest of Hollywood directors, Elia Kazan.

Kazan, like many great artists, was extremely self-effacing, friendly and kind. He was born in Istanbul of Greek parents, and came to the United States as an immigrant child. The irony this particular evening was that next to Kazan was a younger man with a large cast on his foot, who spoke non-stop about Jean-Luc Godard's movies, which is a bit like trying to analyse Taki's works while standing next to Aristophanes. The man in the cast turned out to be one of Godard's assistant directors, and the only thing I can say in his favour is that he had a pretty girl in tow, which is something assistant directors usually do have.

Kazan listened with respect and eventually wandered off. Films like *On the Waterfront*, *A Streetcar Named Desire*, *East of Eden* and *Splendour in the Grass* were obviously never discussed. Not that they should have been. They do, after all, stand up on their own, and no assistant of Kazan's has to remind us of their existence.

I was seated next to Norman's wife, the artist Norris Church, who not only forgave me for being an hour late, she also later forgave me and made me feel at home when I got completely drunk, overstayed my welcome, and babbled on incomprehensibly to one and all.

Opposite me sat Kazan and the funniest English ambassador I've met in a long time. He was straight out of a Durrell novel and, as it turned out, Durrell had served under him while they were both youngsters in the embassy of His Majesty in Egypt at the time. The ambassador had a roving eye, saw Justines left and right, and is an avid reader of the *Spectator*. He asked me about my libel trials, and although this is no time to make jokes about judges, he told such a funny story about two of them, it definitely needs repeating. It seems one judge had just been assigned to a case of aberrant sex, when he casually asked an absentminded colleague of his what he (the colleague) generally gave for sodomy. 'Oh, ten shillings, or whatever change you happen to have on you,' was the answer.

My escort for the evening (the other way round really, as she is the one who asked me to dinner) was Andrea Reynolds, the constant companion of Claus von Bülow, who was in London. Andrea has received almost a million dollars to write about her life with Claus, and about his trial. (For that kind of money I'd gladly live with the girlfriend of the assistant of Godard and hear about him all day.)

Later in the evening my friend Chuck Pfeiffer, Norman and I got into a serious discussion about *King Lear* and boxing, with Mailer making the only sense as he knows both subjects well. Near us I could hear the assistant talking about terrorism, and explaining it away on an intellectual level – which made it obvious that it was time to go. Driving away from Norman's beautiful house and neighbourhood I, too, tried to intellectualize terrorism, but as soon as I bought the morning paper I knew it was a game for mugs. A 17-year-old had just murdered a priest for ten dollars. Enough to buy crack which gives a five-minute high. I then knew I was back in Manhattan and, alas, the real world.

· Immemorial customs ·

Although I've landed at Heathrow many times since that fateful day back on 23 July 1984, my most recent arrival this week brought back the most painful of memories. And even a momentary scare. I thought it a bad omen when I went through immigration in a jiffy (yes, as Max Kelada used to brag, we are all British now, and if anyone dares to call my fellow Greeks wogs, I shall sue) and had my luggage in hand before Alexandra (my ex-wife) was off the airplane. The last time I was out so quickly was on 23 July, and I didn't get far.

Nor did I this time. For a while, anyway. My loving ex had asked me to wait for her before going through customs together – which is a bit like asking Hitler to go to a bar mitzvah – which I did. While I waited I rang up my friend Richard Sykes, and various others not dignified enough to mention, thus missing Alexandra when she came through. After all the passengers had left, I began to worry. All sorts of nightmare scenarios crossed my mind. She might have fainted at the thought that once again she was associating with me. Or been arrested because her father had been to school with Kurt Waldheim. (My ex-papa-in-law told me that Kurt was the stupidest boy in his class, which hardly surprises me; after all, he was the most popular head of the UN for a while.) Worst of all, I imagined she got cold feet before giving evidence on my behalf and grabbed a flight back to the country where they take Teddy Kennedy seriously.

In fact, I was convinced that she had left when I remembered how she encouraged me to go ahead and disembark before her. So I went back up and asked the immigration officer who had seen me through if I might go back inside and search for her. He had a sense of humour. 'I thought you'd be rid of her by now, you were in such a hurry,' was his reply. But the ex was nowhere to be found. One lady official told me to look in the lavatories but not to stay too long, 'otherwise we shall have to arrest you'. (I found only two nice Pakistani lady chars who told me to look in the suitcase, whatever that meant.)

That is when I decided to go through the customs. And guess who was there waiting for me? The two very same officers who had

busted the most persecuted Greek sage since Socrates. 'Hello, Mr Richardson,' was the way I decided to deal with the situation, 'do you remember me?' 'Oooh, Taki,' was the reply, 'of course I do, what have you got on you now?' After exchanging pleasantries for a second or two, Mr Richardson turned inquisitive. 'Why are you so nervous?' he inquired. When I told him about the disappearance of the wife, I felt he became even more suspicious of me. So I left my bags with him and went back inside looking for Madame Godot but to no avail.

But it all turned out for the good. Alexandra had me paged, and when Mr Richardson heard it, out he went looking for her. She later told me that when she saw him approaching her, she literally almost fainted. He's done it again, she told herself, and this time I'll be implicated in all the bad publicity.

Incidentally, the last time I spent the better part of a day with Mr Richardson, he expressed his political leanings in no uncertain terms. This time he told me how a neighbour of his had died and left him £80,000 in his will. For some strange reason I got the impression that his dislike of our present leader had diminished. Probably replaced by a hate for inflation, I imagine.

Nevertheless he could not have been more friendly and polite, and helpful, and he paid me the compliment of not searching me or my luggage, which I hope is a good omen for the coming week.

· Incensed by dwarfs ·

I first heard the rumours about six months ago. John Aspinall was going to throw a party in honour of the Torgamba Forest Sumatran rhinoceros, one of the rarest animals in the world, and now on the brink of extinction. (A catching expedition has been organized by Aspers to rescue some of the remaining rhinos whose natural habitat is being turned into a rubber plantation.) Knowing Aspinall as I do, it didn't surprise me. Normal people give parties for their daughter's coming out, or wedding, or even their son's coming of age. Although his 60th birthday passed unnoticed last month, Aspers has yet to celebrate a living human. It is either great kings of the past, or noble animals of the present.

This time rumour had it that 1,000 Mesopotamian midgets would be flown to Kent in order to *épater les bourgeois*. But as usual, the rumour-mongers got it wrong. There were only 24 of them, and they all turned out to be dwarfs, and all holders of British passports to boot. The other thing the rumour-reapers didn't guess was that the Torgamba party of last Saturday will probably do for future party givers what the Ligne Maginot did for French national pride in May 1940. Let me explain.

At the age of 48 I feel I've been around long enough to know about parties and balls as well as, say, Lord Elgin knew the importance of saving marbles from uncivilized environments and preserving them for posterity. Some of the great ones that come to mind were the Bestegui one in Venice, the Agnelli dance in the Bois de Boulogne, the last party the Rothschilds gave at their château at Ferrière, and the Patino blast in Portugal during the final years of Salazar. And although it may sound ungracious to compare, such was the spectacle Aspinall created last Saturday that I'm sure my hosts of the past will understand. This put them all to shame.

The ball took place at Port Lympne, Hythe, the Sir Herbert Baker-built mansion for Sir Philip Sassoon, now owned by Aspers. I arrived promptly at 8.45 and, as parking attendants took my car, we were greeted by the scarlet-tunicked Queen's Regiment band that struck up the kind of military marches that can inspire even a Lebanese to act nobly. Then it was about a mile's walk through what Russell Page has called the most beautiful gardens in England, and Rex Whistler, the Virgin Forest. It was through stands of catalpa trees over 40 feet high, accompanied by wolves, Siberian tigers and a snow leopard or two that one suddenly arrived at the Great Stairs that lead down to the house.

On either side of the Trojan stairway are cascading boxed hedges, giving a pyramid, or ziggurat, effect. Five years ago Aspinall had chosen boy scouts to line the stairs and entrance. This time, the theme being the rhino, Michael Howell had created a Sumatran market scene that was, well, as real as any Sumatran market scene would be if directed by Cecil B. De Mille in the good old days of Hollywood. There were half-naked, exotically dressed 'Sumatrans', pelting us with rose petals, offering us food, while the dwarfs stirred their cups and produced the strongest smell of incense I've smelt outside the Greek Orthodox Church.

Down at the bottom of the Nuremberg-like stairway stood Aspinall and Sally greeting their by now rather open-mouthed guests. Every person there was known to the Aspinalls, all 432 of us, which is a rarity in itself. Hosts today invite people for what they are – especially in America – and the guests are the important element of the party. Not Aspinall. With him, his guests serve as an audience, or necessary extras, to his creative megalomania. In fact, he reminded me of a Renaissance prince, greeting the people who were paying homage to his genius for living well. Small-minded people like the Hartleys of this world may call it a waste, but that would be as wrong as calling Carter-Ruck an aristocrat.

Dinner, needless to say, was seated, and the tent had been transformed into a tropical rain forest by Michael Howell, who had spent four months planning the details. The seating followed a racist theme, or a racist aspect, rather. Better yet, it was vintage Aspinall. There were his Greek friends, their voices now lowered because of the crash of the shipping market, all seated together. Then there were the Sephardic Jews, happy to be once again making money in the countries of their choice, and the South African Jews, looking worried, but happy for a night. There was also the noisy racing owners table, with their acolytes, and the nob table, presided over by my cousin Sunny Marlborough and including Lords Warwick and Suffolk. And there was the jailbird table, with Justin Frewen, Taki and someone who almost made it but didn't.

Aspers never was a man to forsake old friends, whatever misfortune may have engulfed them, and they were there too. Last but not least was the homosexual table, headed by the octogenarian who survived the sinking of the *Titanic* by dressing up as a girl and screaming, 'Mommy, Mommy.' (There were eight poofters among the 432.) Oh, I almost forgot, there was also the Westminster table, headed by a government minister and the best-looking MP in the Commons, both of whom showed interest in prison reform and questioned me closely.

After the cabaret we retired to the north lawn where Robert Tear, accompanied by the Philharmonic Orchestra, sang the favourite songs of another great tenor, Richard Tauber. I sat in front with my NBF, Benjy Fraser, and Natasha Grenfell and suddenly realized how Mrs Thatcher could do away once and for all with drug addiction, thuggery, Aids, and other diseases too ghastly to mention. All she has to do is ban rock music, jail every rock star except for Harry Worcester, and *c'est tout*.

Everyone's mood was so uplifted by the music that if somebody had offered anyone a snort, or a joint, they would have been as welcome as a Democrat in the Kremlin. Afterwards we danced to the Neal Smith band from Palm Beach, and the newest song they played was written before the war. I danced for the first time in 20 years, and danced non-stop for close to six hours. As always, I was the last person to leave, and continued at the Imperial Hotel, which Aspers had taken over for his guests. But Aspers told me that in five years he'll do it again and, knowing how preposterous and sumptuous he can be, I wouldn't put it past him.

· Reduced circumstances ·

As some of you may have surmised, the greatest Greek since Melina Mercouri has suddenly become the poorest Greek since Diogenes. (A jury had awarded substantial damages against Taki, the defendant, in a celebrated libel suit.) I realized how bad things were when I stopped by the *Literary Review*'s offices the other day in order to buy a subscription, and Auberon Waugh instructed his extremely attractive assistant only to accept cash. Mr Waugh obviously knows the difference between being bankrupt and being broke.

But not to worry. Being broke will probably make me a better scribe, and I will finally be able to write about the human condition and other important matters. No more stuff about drunken nights at Annabel's, no more front-line reporting from Gstaad's Palace, not a word about high jinks from private islands in Greece. From now on it will be Coach and Horses stories, and how Jeff shared his last vodka and lime with the poor little Greek.

Mind you, I hope still to be invited by my posh friends (Jeff's words, not mine) when their daughters or sisters get hitched, or when they decide to blow half a million in order to celebrate a monkey's trip from Sumatra to Kent. And speaking of going bust, I read that Adnan Khashoggi, a man who only last year was reputed to be the richest in the world, may soon be joining me in penury. If he does, I'm sure he will be going bankrupt, not broke, and I'm willing to bet Jeff's recent win on that. I first met Khashoggi when I was richer than he. He came to Gstaad and a friend of mine, Arnaud de Borchgrave, had him to dinner. I found him as charming as he was unpleasing to look at, a fat and short little man who looked 20 years older than he was. Khashoggi eventually made his pile by becoming the Mr Five Per Cent for the Saudi ruling princes. The pile grew and grew until finally Adnan lost his way and began to believe what his PR people were feeding the hacks. His opulent lifestyle, however, made the Saudis nervous. They began to distance themselves from him just about when Khomeini started to kill people. Then came hubris. Adnan struck out on his own, wheeling and dealing and trying to control the resources of whole countries. The Sudan proved his undoing (as it did for my ancestor, Chinese Gordon). Once Numeiri was deposed, Adnan's deal went the way of Libyan democracy. Which I guess shows that the days when the United Fruit Company of America could ask and get the United States to invade Guatemala are over.

Now Adnan is in a cash squeeze, and I hear his £90-million yacht as well as one of his three DC9s is up for sale. Adnan needs $10 million per month to live, which means he has a lot of catching up to do if he's to join Jeff and Taki in our barrel. (Diogenes lived in one, and I'm actually contemplating buying one.)

Which brings me back to my own problems. I wonder what the sainted one will call my column now that I can no longer afford to write from such exotic places as Spetsopoula, Porto Heli, and Scorpios. (For any of you who have never heard of these places, they are leper islands for extremely rich white trash in the Aegean archipelago.) Perhaps 'Low life' and 'Home life' should be followed by 'Dog's life'. When my daddy read about my losses in the Greek newspapers he rang and told me he was sure no jury would ever rule in my favour because of my abrasive personality and ghastly lifestyle. My saintly mother, on the other hand, wrote to me that she had lit a candle for me and that had I done the same I would have won. (I had, and didn't.)

· In the swim ·

Athens · It doesn't make sense, but the older the shipowner, the faster the boat. Take Evanghelos Nomikos, for example. He was very rich and always owned magnificent boats which he kept selling, and ordering newer and faster ones. Towards the end of his life he owned the fastest boat in the Med, but he hardly ever took her out of the harbour.

Stavros Niarchos made his money after the second world war, and immediately bought *Eros*, a black two-masted ketch, and the most beautiful sailing boat ever, the three-masted *Creole*. But the moment he became 65 he started cruising on stinkpots, and enormous and fast stinkpots at that. Even Gianni Agnelli, the charismatic Fiat chairman, switched from sails – he once owned a boat that didn't even have an auxiliary engine – to pistons, once on the wrong side of 40. My old man, ditto. Our two-masted ketch, the *Aries*, was the toughest boat I've ever travelled on, and we sure travelled back then. Afterwards he bought the *Nefertiti*, and I the *Bushido*, two of the best-looking sailing boats around, but now we are reduced to only one large and extremely expensive gas-guzzler, which can cruise at 35 knots, and which sleeps ten in comfort.

But, as I said, the speed doesn't make sense. My father is now 79 years old, and spends four days a week on board, but going nowhere. Here is what he does. He rings up my mother every Friday morning and asks her whether she'd like to go with him for the weekend. As she has done for some 30-odd years, she declines and wishes him a pleasant trip. He then calls up some of his friends, and steams out of the harbour and heads for Angistri, a mere 22 miles away. After reaching his destination in less than one hour he orders the captain to drop anchor, his cook to start cooking, and goes for a two-hour swim. On Monday evening he heads back to port. None of his friends seem to complain, but I've got my doubts. And it's probably the reason the girls keep getting younger and younger. After all, nobody of mature or voting age would put up with simply watching a man swim for four days straight.

I spent all last week on board, anchored off Angistri and, thank

God, the ex-wife and my two children were on board (plus a young girl who my father insisted was his new assistant). I used to love to swim, but no longer. Even in out of the way islands the sea is too polluted, and anyway it doesn't give me the kind of rush I feel after an hour's karate, or a boxing match, or even a long run.

This week is my birthday, and I've now begun the countdown to

50. In 364 days I shall reach that depressing age, but I plan to enjoy myself until then. It is a bit distressing, but not as much as when I realized that my reflexes are completely gone and that all sorts of nonentities simply come up to me and whack me at will. The old man has now turned against karate, and thinks I'm much too old for it. I disagree. If he can surround himself with young girls, I certainly can fight with young men. Anyway, I'm sure that the reflexes may just pay me a visit in September when I'll be at Crystal Palace for karate week.

On the last day we were anchored off that rock a friend of my father's tied up next to us, so at least we had some company. The wife of my father's friend is a legend in Greece. She's absent-minded but extremely pleasant and quick. She's also a rarity in this part of the world, a true lady. Alexandra told her a story which took place in Gstaad and involved yours truly. Christine Ockrent, a French television interviewer with politics like those of Scargill's, and therefore an old adversary of mine, greeted me one day by saying, '*Bonjour* Taki, *toujours fasciste*?' to which I answered, '*Bonjour* Christine, *toujours putain*?'

That reminded the lady of an incident that took place in Athens when she ran into an acquaintance of hers and, as was the custom at the time, asked her in French, '*Et comment va votre marie*?' when she suddenly realized that the husband had been dead for a year. So in desperation she blurted out, '*Toujours mort*?' The same lady was the Greek ambassadress to Madrid when she had to attend a lying-in-state for a diplomat who had just joined that embassy in the sky. When she entered the house she handed her new flowered hat to the butler and then paid her respects to the deceased. Suddenly to her horror she saw her hat at the feet of the dead man – as the butler had mistaken it for a tray of flowers. As she told us last week, she cried for the dead man, but also for her hat. Well, there is nothing like old family tales to help pass the time away, especially when one has to sit on the fastest boat in the Aegean and watch a man swim round and round.

· The Bounder ·

As everyone who has ever heard of the Pampas knows, Louis Basualdo is the Argentinian polo professional who eloped with Lord Cowdray's teenage daughter back in the early Seventies, thus establishing himself as the undisputed *numero uno* of bounders among the practitioners of a sport known to contain more cads than Jeffrey Bernard has had hangovers, and then some. Needless to say, as soon as his infant bride became pregnant, all was forgiven, and Basualdo became as much of a fixture around Cowdray Park as, say, Lord Cowdray's helicopter. Basualdo did not let his new-found wealth go to his head. One of his first acts was to recruit the Prince of Wales as back in his team, the Golden Eagles. His recruitment of the prince was a fruitful one, and it is known even among those who have never heard of the game, that Basualdo's inside pockets are lined with pictures of himself and the heir to the throne. Later on, Basualdo publicly presented the Prince with a gift pony flown in especially for the occasion by the bounder from the Pampas, a pony that Basualdo's Boswell, Nigel Dempster, later claimed to have been an Argentinian donkey in disguise, but that is a different matter altogether.

Those halcyon days did not last long, however. After about five years of marriage, Lucy Basualdo had had enough. She sued for divorce, the grounds being cruelty, flagrant debauchery, and not a small amount of adultery. Basualdo resisted, but just before the juiciest of divorce cases was to be heard, Lord Cowdray offered, and Basualdo reluctantly accepted, £200,000.

I had known Basualdo before his marriage – when he was after Christina Onassis, which proved to me he was a brave man – but after his divorce from Lucy I befriended him. The English contingent had dropped him like the proverbial hot potato, so I figured it was time to be seen with him in public. Which I did for a long time. I enjoyed his company and still do, although his constant meddling in other people's business has caused me not a small number of problems.

Others, however, found his gossiping to be too vicious, and impossible to accept. When he rented a cottage and moved to Beaufort

Hunt country, his presence was met with alarm. When he bought two hunters, and appeared in top hat and immaculate hunting pink with his factotum Ludovico in attendance, people broke and ran. One of our most distinguished historians, Princess Michael of Kurtz, was among the first to complain of his presence. Finally the Duke of Beaufort had to give in to popular demand and refuse him the blue and buff. Basualdo hit back by spreading more rumours than Princess Michael has lifted passages. What followed was inevitable.

Sometime after lunch two weeks ago, Major Ronald Ferguson received a call from a man he hadn't heard from in years. 'Hi, Ron, this is Louis Basualdo,' said the voice. Ferguson immediately went on guard. 'What do you want?' asked the good major. 'I was thinking about playing at Windsor next year,' answered the voice, to which Ferguson immediately said, 'Absolutely not, we don't need your kind here,' and was about to hang up when the voice said, 'Too bad, Ronny, because I have certain pictures of Fergie which the press might be very interested in.'

To Major Ferguson's eternal credit, he slammed the telephone down and that is where the matter ended, as far as he's concerned. But word got out that the Bounder had tried to pull a number on the father of the Duchess of York, and all hell broke loose. Fergie herself is said to be furious, and demanding the Bounder's head. I don't know what the major's plans are, as I don't even know for certain that the call ever took place. But if it did, I know that Basualdo's was not the voice on the telephone. For once he is innocent of all charges.

But at Sir Gordon White's dinner dance for 500 of his closest friends last Saturday, the Bounder looked pale, without his usual man-tan makeup, and his behaviour was that of a broken man. Nothing like a practical joke at one's expense to turn even an irrepressible character like the Bounder into a social lamb. I now predict the Bounder will leave these islands for ever, and I for one will miss him.

1987

· Good time girls ·

New York · Well, one more year has gone the way of Ivan Boesky, and ever since New Year's Day my liver has been acting as if it was about to be indicted for insider trading. The beginning of the end – for my liver, that is – was Christmas Eve, when I had 60 of my closest and dearest for dinner at my house, and it continued up to and including New Year's Day, when I finally collapsed in Long Island with the kind of hangover that killed my ancestor Alexander the Great long ago.

As I am neither *nouveau riche*, nor a social climber, I will not list the people who came to dinner – something that is *de rigueur* over here among the 'beautiful people' – I will simply mention that never have so many brains been in one room at the same time. There was a table for the brainy ones, another for the women and social types, and a third for those who had youth. Needless to say, and by popular demand, I sat with the brains, between John Gross and Professor Ernest van den Haag, to be exact, but eventually ceded my place when the Professor demanded that Carolina Herrera sit next to him instead of the greatest Greek since George Papadopoulos.

And speaking of Carolina Herrera, I am willing to bet the Caravel Hotel in Athens (the loser gets to keep it) that there is no more beautiful mother-daughter combination in the civilized world. Carolina *mère* looks like Rita Hayworth before she knew the ghastly Ali Khan, and Carolina *fille*, well, words fail me. But let me try. I watched her as she entered the dining-room and smiled at everyone. The summery tint of her bare arms ... the indistinct tenderness of her still narrow but already not quite flat chest ... the folds of her skirt ... their succinctness and soft concavities ... her brushing against me with a bare elbow, invoked an intolerable sensation of sanguine, dermal, multivascular communion with her. OK, OK, so it's Vladimir Nabokov, but Taki suffers just as much whenever he sees either of the Carolinas.

After dinner I gave a speech thanking my guests for not having gone to Nell's as soon as the food had run out, and after my speech – in fact, during – that is exactly what most of them did, including yours truly. Although the last time I wrote about Nell's I made a few pejorative remarks about the place, I can now safely say that I have logged more hours in the joint than Nell herself. Incidentally, Nell must either be Australian or she must have gone to Eton, because she has a great sense of humour and did not hold it against me. What she does hold against me is the fact that I stuck Anthony Haden-Guest with the bill one night, and Anthony paid it with one of his . . . personal cheques. In fact, Nell's has now replaced Annabel's as far as my favourite club is concerned, at least while I'm in the Big Bagel.

So Nell's it was every night up until New Year's Eve, and then it was Reinaldo Herrera's turn to do the honours. I, needless to say, had the best seat in the house, as I sat between Carolina *fille* and her step-sister. I ate nothing but drank a lot and sighed even more. While she ate I thought to myself that for the glow of her cheeks, the 12 pairs of narrow ribs, her wisp of a soul, the unknown thoughts that were running through her head, for all this I would have given a sack of rubies, a bucket of blood, anything I was asked.

Yes, yes, I know, it's Vladimir again, but I swear I did think such thoughts. Then the mother of my children told me to stop sighing so loudly, and to give a speech because it was 5 a.m. and the Herreras wanted to go to bed. I did exactly that, and in no time I found myself at Nell's until the mother of my children telephoned and ordered Nell to send me home.

The reason I had such a wonderful time during Christmas week was obvious. The 'beautiful people' had gone underground as there are no charity functions and even their press agents take a rest. So, instead of reading about the Gutfreunds, the de la Rentas and the Zipkins of this world, I passed my evenings admiring the two Carolinas, their breathing, their legs, their hair, everything they did . . . I know, I know, it's that damn Russian again, but I swear that's why I had such a good time.

· Tough times ·

New York · I first heard of pleurisy in the summer of 1962, during a cruise off the Côte d'Azur, when the widow of a famous French dress designer came down with it. We anchored off St Tropez and sent for a doctor, who came on board and diagnosed it. As soon as she heard, she asked him where it came from. 'It comes from the Greek,' answered the kind physician. 'Oh, that son-of-a-bitch,' roared the widow.

I thought of old Genevieve last week when a New York doctor defined what ails yours truly as pleurisy. But, unlike her, I didn't blame any of the friends I've made recently. It seems that our lungs are enclosed in a double bag called the pleura, and pleurisy is an inflammation of this bag. The symptoms are a sudden, severe, stabbing pain in the side or shoulder, aggravated by breathing or coughing. To laugh is pure agony.

I had been training rather hard in the weeks following my Christmas and New Year's celebrations, and at first thought the pain was from a blow I had received. It got progressively worse, and finally the mother of my children rang for the doctor, who gave me the bad news. He prescribed a prolonged rest and convalescence, plus a lot of antibiotics. I ain't got time for the former and the latter make me feel like a radical socialist, i.e. lousy.

I had planned to finish my Ballad of Pentonville Jail in two weeks, and then fly to Australia, where the editor of the *Sydney Morning Herald* has kindly invited me to cover the shenanigans that will surely take place when that boring Dennis Connor tries to recapture the America's Cup. Now, I'm not so sure I'll make it to the birthplace of Homer, Shakespeare, Goethe, Mozart, Lew Hoad, Neale Fraser, and Bob Hughes. And 'tis a pity. I was truly looking forward to mingling with the *aficionados* in Perth, and cheering the Aussies to victory. But before anyone gets the wrong idea, let me explain why.

Unlike most people who have benefited from America, I am not a knee-jerk anti-American. In fact, I have rooted against America only twice before. The first time it was when Ecuador, South America's most distinguished country, was playing the US in the Davis

Cup. The Ecuadorians were Guzman and Zuleta. My friend was Zuleta, who is pitch black, small, probably tubercular, but with more guts than all the Arab states put together. Zuleta and I had travelled the tennis circuit together during the Sixties, and he had always tried to help me out by playing doubles with me, and giving me tips on the game. Zuleta had no backhand, no volley, no serve, and he could not hit an overhead. I had all those strokes, yet he managed to win consistently, and I to lose.

Zuleta became famous among the players when he ran off and married a beautiful Swedish girl during a tournament. I remember explaining to some of the female players – who were dumbfounded, to say the least – what Zuleta's attributes were. 'If you'd seen him in the showers, you'd understand,' was the way I believe I put it.

So, when Zuleta and the even smaller Guzman faced the giant from the north, I had to root for my old doubles partner. And believe it or not, the Ecuadorians beat the gringos. Mind you, I presume there must have been some close calls, and I heard the crowd was not exactly a sporting one, but it was nevertheless a famous victory. Zuleta was given a banana stand by the dictator of Ecuador in appreciation, and Guzman's father was let out of jail. This was back in 1967 or '68, I believe, but I could have my dates wrong.

The second time I rooted against Uncle Sam was in 1983, when the Aussies won the America's Cup. Although at the time I had yet to sell my soul to John Fairfax, I rooted against my father's club – the NYYC – because I thought their tactics were as close as they could get to cheating within the rules. I also found Dennis Connor to be a bore. In fact, Connor is to charm what Roy Hattersley is to anorexia.

He is, however, a hell of a sailor, and the land of Aristotle, Socrates, Roy Emerson and Nigel Dempster will have a tough time keeping the Cup. If I'm still in bed I'll watch it on the telly, otherwise I'll be there, looking like a Greek Greta Garbo, coughing and holding my chest.

· Stylish visitors ·

New York · Nothing makes one feel as well as feeling normal after having been ill. Just as nothing makes one feel more ill than training after having been idle for a week or two. My two one-time students, Elias and Dimitri Kazakeas, both third dan black belts, arrived to stay with me last Sunday, and we've been kicking and punching each other non-stop. Dimitri won the Greek national championship last year, and my sore ribs are proof that his victory was no fluke. But despite the pain it's great to be fighting again, if only in the gym and between friends.

There was yet another sudden arrival, namely that of 'l'Avvocato', who to the world at large is none other than Giovanni Agnelli, chairman of Fiat, the Turin-based automotive giant. I have often written about Gianni, and have always described him as charismatic, very attractive, extremely intelligent and charming – adjectives I like to think I don't easily throw around, especially when writing about men as rich and powerful as he is.

But he is all that and much more, and I had as much fun spending three evenings in his company as I have practising karate in the Dojo. Gianni and I have been friends for almost 30 years, without ever having had an argument or a misunderstanding, a record of sorts in view of my volatile character. On the first night I hardly drew a breath while regaling everyone with some of the fun we've had in the past.

Although nostalgia embellishes stories even more than I do, I truly can't think of ever having had a better time than when the present Duke of Beaufort, Gianni and I took a month-long cruise from the Riviera to Greece in the company of a famous striptease artist, Erica Nielsen. Whenever we'd run into bores – and we ran into quite a few – Erica would be presented as a great lady and then she would begin doing her act and the bores would flee. It worked until the crew almost mutinied. They had not, after all, seen a woman for some time, and despite her advanced age, la Nielsen was quite sexy. I haven't seen her for years, but I hope she's still alive and well. The last I heard of her she was in Mexico, keeping company with Loel Guinness.

On Gianni's second night we met in his flat on Park Avenue and watched the last race of the America's Cup. While we waited for the race to start, I confirmed something I had suspected for a long time. He had once, when I had asked him what his definition of style was, told me about an incident he had witnessed. The incident took place in Libya during the second world war. It seems there was an attractive German officer sitting in a Tripoli bar one night in the company of a Levantine lady of the night, of rare beauty. While enjoying their drinks they were approached by a young and good-looking Italian cavalry officer who politely began to flirt with the lady. The German gent was also polite – after all, they were allies – until the Italian gently put his arm around the lady's shoulders. That is when the German, without saying a word, took out his pistol and very discreetly winged the Italian's arm, thus removing it from her.

All three were sitting, and there was a lot of noise, and no one realized where the shot had come from. They finished their drinks, and then the Italian excused himself and smilingly left the room. I remember that at the time Gianni had told me the story, I had thought that both the German and the Italian had shown great style. Gianni had said the German had shown more. Now I know why: 'l'Avvocato' was the Italian officer who got shot.

· Warhol's put-ons ·

New York · Andy Warhol and I suffered from the same social disease. We both needed to go out to a party every night. When the news came in last Sunday that Andy was dead, I hoped against hope that he might have sent a double to the hospital for gallstone surgery, and that the real Warhol would show up that night in New York but it was not to be. As of this writing, Andy's tragic and untimely death is still a mystery.

He was born Andrew Warhola, the son of a Czech miner-immigrant who died when Andy was only 14. He somehow scraped the money together and attended the Carnegie Institute of Technology in Pittsburgh, graduating in 1949 with a degree in pictorial design. He moved to the Big Apple, cut the final vowel from his name, and quickly found success as a commercial artist.

Ten years after graduating, however, Warhol got bored and began painting in earnest. He never looked back. What he did was revolutionary to some, and a fraud to others, but there was no question that he was instrumental in extending what the public accepted as art. Marilyn Monroe, Brillo boxes, Elvis Presley, cans of soup, Dick Tracy, and the rich and famous all became his subjects, but what really sold Warhols was Andy himself. His forte was the fun he poked at the art world, the constant put-ons, the ambiguity of it all.

He was a fixture of New York nightlife, attending every party, every opening, always surrounded by a group he called his 'superstars'. I knew most of them, but my close friend was his very first 'superstar', Baby Jane Holzer. Her discovery was typical and pure Warhol. Jane was an overweight, rich Jewish princess from the wrong side of Park Avenue. She had trouble with her weight, her parents, but most of all with men. One day, outside Bloomingdale's (where else) she was spotted by Andy. 'There's a very mysterious woman,' whispered Andy. Jane Holzer was as mysterious as a nail file, in fact she was like all the other million-odd Jewish princesses in the city, but Warhol was adamant. She became his first 'superstar'.

And the master of the put-on got away with it. Baby Jane Holzer was soon on every chic magazine cover, and no event could be called

a happening unless she and her Svengali were present. That was back in the middle Sixties, and Jane was soon followed by Edie Sedwick, the society girl who died from a heroin overdose. Andy got a bum rap on that one. Edie was a druggie long before he made her a star. Warhol never touched drugs, alcohol or tobacco, nor did he encourage them.

Warhol's other put-ons were legion. The one I preferred was his film of a man sleeping for 30 straight hours. He was the most prolific artist of his time, making movies, writing books, publishing *Interview* magazine, hosting cable-TV shows, and painting enough portraits and pictures to fill galleries and museums. And he went out. Every night, and loved it. Especially the glamour of it all. He knew every celebrity in the world, and every celebrity knew him. But it never went to his head.

I used to see him during those wild days of the Sixties, always watching, never speaking, always extremely polite and deferring to others. 'Wow, that's great,' was his favourite expression. He was the most soft-spoken of men, as well as the nicest. In 1968, a deranged feminist shot him. The bullet passed into his left lung, abdomen and chest, and hit his spleen, liver and oesophagus before exiting on the right side. He lay close to death for two months, but never pressed charges. It was after the shooting that he began sending doubles to certain events. At one time I thought there must have been at least as many Warhols making the rounds as there were Warhol groupies.

He was a devout Catholic and a very loving son. He is survived by two brothers, both of whom still live in Pennsylvania as blue-collar workers. It is usual to finish eulogies by saying how much the recently deceased will be missed. More often than not people are not missed at all. Andy will be, not only by the hundreds who benefited from him, but by those who live at night, like myself, who know that the only originals left in this world are to be found at night, Andy's favourite time. He was also my employer for the last two years, which shows that Andy made fun of the literary world, too.

· Night owls ·

New York · This is my last week in the Big Bagel. By the time you read this I hope to be skiing with the Buckleys in Gstaad, and doing some social work among the rich. My plan is to fly to Zurich first, where I will attend a conference and hear a speech by my old buddy Arnaud de Borchgrave, the editor of the *Washington Times*, and then Arnaud and I will go up to the Palace for some badly needed rest and recreation.

Arnaud and I have been travelling together for some 20 years now. It was he who told me that the best way to find girls was to be a member of the press, and I have been thanking him ever since. In fact, I've just published a profile of Arnaud in the American *Spectator*, in which I detail exactly how much I owe the man as far as the fair sex is concerned.

Travelling with Arnaud, and about to go skiing with William and Christopher Buckley is the good news, but I got the bad news yesterday when I rang the Palace Hotel and asked to speak to my oldest friend, John Zographos. He has cancelled his reservation, I was told, and somehow Gstaad will not be Gstaad without him. In fact, it will be the first time since 1952 that Zographos will not be taking up space – and lots of it – in the Palace bar, in the Greengo, or the first table on the right of the terrace in the Eagle Club.

Now, although some of you may find this a bit distasteful, I feel I ought to tell loyal *Spectator* readers how Zographos and I first met. It was in 1953, the year President and Field Marshal Papagos decreed that all brothels in Greece should be shut down. Needless to say, not any of them did, although the girls did stop soliciting from their windows and balconies, especially when the fuzz was around.

The best whorehouse in town was Zoitsa's near Omonia Square, where the *soi disant* Athenian aristocracy spent their afternoons. I already had a taste of this life the summer before on the French Riviera, but was eager as hell to find out if the Greeks were as good as the Frogs. I had never met Zographos – as he is much, much older than I am – but I had heard stories about his expert knowledge of the world's oldest profession.

On a hot afternoon, after lunch and before a tennis match, I went down to Zoitsa's and rang the bell. Greek brothels were required by law to have green doors, and once they became illegal, they all painted their doors a different colour. I remember it well because some of the paint stuck on my eager hand. After a while a blonde lady appeared from a window on the second floor and asked me to state my business. Having had a proper education, I wasn't about to tell her what I really wanted, so I said I was a friend of Zographos and was expecting him at this address. 'Oh, he's here already,' said the madame, and buzzed me in.

Well, you can guess the rest. Zographos was busy, but as soon as I asked for a girl, the madame got frightened because I was under-age, and worse, looked it. So she went in and got Zog out of bed and told him that what he was doing was dangerous, and he lost his temper because he was slightly drunk and hadn't the foggiest what she was talking about.

The comedy of errors had a happy ending, however. Zog knew my name, and when I shyly told him why I had used his in vain, he opened a bottle of warm champagne, toasted me, and then proceeded to pay for my pleasant afternoon. He thought it was my first time, and wanted to make sure there was no trauma. We were later in the navy together, and have remained best friends ever since.

Four years ago Zographos did the dirty on me and got married, and he's been blissfully happy ever since. He is now a father, a good husband and a country squire, although he does tend to scare the horses when he goes stalking around the English countryside in a double-breasted pin-striped suit.

I forgave Zog for getting married, and even forgave him when he settled down, but I don't think I shall forgive, nor forget, his not coming to Gstaad this year. I love skiing with the Buckleys, and listening to them talk – whenever they can get a word in – but they do suffer from the most bourgeois habit of all: they go to sleep at night. Zog never used to, and I still don't. I wonder what kind of company the snow makes at night?

· Royal cactus ·

Gstaad · Although some readers might suspect I'm on the take from the Swiss office of tourism, if anything it is the other way around. However broke I find myself after my yearly visit to good old Helvetia, I simply cannot stop raving about the country Papa Hemingway described as more upside down than sideways.

As an American might say, the place just blows my mind. It is not only among the most beautiful countries on earth, it is also the cleanest. It is committed to unbridled capitalism, yet it follows socialist principles. Its trade unions are rich and powerful, but also extremely responsible. Finally, every able-bodied man up to the age of 55 is armed to the teeth, yet the crime rate is the lowest anywhere.

Looking back at the 32 years that I've been going to Switzerland, the past ten days must rank among the happiest. It obviously had to do with the company I kept. Oh, yes, the snow was also perfect, and the sun shone every day but one. My day began with 15 kilometres of cross-country skiing, followed by a long liquid lunch *chez les* Buckleys, the Eagle Club, or in the terrace of a trout restaurant near Gsteig, and ended with three hours of downhill skiing in Rougemont or the Wassengrat. After embarrassing myself in the Eagle Club race last week, I stuck to uncompetitive stuff, which – not surprisingly – turned out to be much more fun. I guess the real meaning of getting old is accepting it, and I now accept the fact that I shall never try to compete again. In skiing, that is.

My nights were spent in the company of Christopher Buckley and his wife Lucy, my friend Mario Ruspoli – a man who makes Pol Pot seem the epitome of compassion – and an old flame from my Swiss past. I accepted only two dinner invitations during my ten days' stay, and that seems to be the trick of finding happiness in the Alps. There is a lot of rich white trash in Gstaad, and even some that's not so white (the Lebanese) and if one goes to parties one is bound to get stuck next to some of them.

Christopher and Lucy are the most delightful companions, mainly because they're attractive and intelligent, but also because they allow one to speak, however non-stop. Prince Ruspoli is another matter.

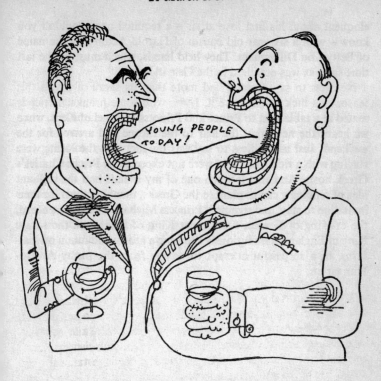

He hates the modern world far more than I do, and spends his time complaining about it. Ten minutes with him is like five hours at a Nuremberg rally. I suspect the Buckleys cut their holiday short after one night when both Ruspoli and I went over the top. But – as Barnaby Conrad said – it was fun while it lasted.

And then, of course, there was the sage of Château d'Oex, Alastair Forbes, better known as Gotha Forbes to us Swiss *aficionados*. Both my invitations to dine were turned down by my favourite book reviewer, on the grounds that he preferred to burn the midnight oil getting through a brilliant 850-page book sent to him by his pinko Vietnam-veteran nephew, John Forbes Kerry, the junior senator from Massachusetts, a man who I suspect reads less than a predecessor in that seat, his uncle's one-time pal, J. F. Kennedy. Ali regaled me instead with stories about the Gstaad of 60 years ago, when there were no ski-lifts, and only one car, the doctor's. He waxed eloquent about his first love affair – a requited one, wouldn't you know – with a six-year-old cousin of Harold Acton's by the name of Betty Lou Dillingham. They held hands, which must be the last time safe sex was practised in the Gstaad Palace.

Needless to say, Gstaad had more than its share of royals this season. As luck would have it, I was with some prankster friends seated at a table next to Prince and Princess Michael of Kent, when we heard the news that the heir to the throne had arrived for the weekend. Just as needless to say was the fact that the Kents were staying with a rich Arab, and were not expected by Prince Charles's Greek hosts. And that is when one of my friends had the brilliant idea of sending a cactus plant to the Greeks, thanking them for their invitation to stay, and signing it Princess Michael. The last we heard, the ex-King of Greece, the present King of Spain and the future King of England were furiously climbing a nearby mountain on seal-skins, in a successful attempt to escape from the pushy Austro-Hungarian.

· Unromantic Atlantic ·

New York · Last Monday I heard a sound that reminded me not only of my happy youth, but also of a time when one travelled for the sheer joy of it.

Avvocato Agnelli had just flown in and we had gone for a walk along the Riverside when we heard the sound. It was distant, and faint, but it was the customary three long rumbling hoots of an ocean liner's whistle as it departed from the 55th Street terminal on New York's West Side. Hearing them made us spend the rest of the morning talking yet again about the good old days.

As a schoolboy, I crossed the Atlantic regularly during the summer holidays, leaving New York some time in July and returning the first week in September. Back in the early Fifties everyone on holiday travelled by ship, while only foreign correspondents, spies, and the Boeskys of the time preferred to fly. Needless to say, there were more girls on board those sun liners – as they were called – than there are self-serving, emotional and extremely boring speeches in Hollywood during the Academy awards.

The most beautiful girl I ever met on board a ship was a Texan by the name of Isla Cowan. She was blonde, tall, with a Kim Basinger body, a Texas accent, and the reputation of being one of the richest girls of the Lone Star State. I was 15 to her 16, dark, short, poor, but as determined to conquer her as Santa Anna was to take the Alamo. Oh, yes, I almost forgot, I was not so poor on that trip, because I was travelling on my own. My parents were already in Europe and were meeting me in Cannes, which meant I could sign for everything I drank, and for everything others drank, too.

I was seated at Captain Jacobsen's table for my meals, as were the Cowans, those good old days being élitist and the captain not having to eat with everyone who could afford a first-class ticket. I made it a point to offer the captain and the Cowans non-stop champagne, and my ploy worked. Everyone thought I was a millionaire who simply looked much younger than his years.

Of course, it all ended in tears. Once we dropped anchor in Cannes and my father came on board to collect me, all hell broke loose.

Upon seeing the bills I had signed he began to shout, and demanded to see the captain who had allowed it. Worse, he told Captain Jacobsen and the Cowans what a phoney I was. I remember having my last supper at the captain's table next to my father, and seeing Isla looking at me in the manner in which I imagine my old friend Joan Collins must be contemplating the bloated face of her ex across the courtroom just about now. Hell hath no fury like a beautiful woman taken for a ride.

After I left school I continued to cross by ocean liners, the most memorable being in 1957, 7 March to be precise, when Leonidas Goulandris, John Zographos and I took the *Liberté* from Le Havre for New York. Each of us had a suite, and entertained high hopes of romance on the high seas. The *Liberté* was truly a beauty, with the most wonderful panelling and grand salons. What it lacked on that particular trip was women. There were 80 Venezuelan businessmen on board, and *c'est tout*. Zographos went down to steerage and found a German girl who looked as if she hadn't had a bath since the Berlin blockade four years earlier. He upgraded her to first, took her to dinner in the private first-class dining-room, where Goulandris was sick all over her. While she went to the lavatory to clean up, a drunken Venezuelan assaulted her, and the three of us went to her rescue. I had a broken leg at the time, so I used my crutches against the South American brutes, bending one of my sticks against the hard head of the rapist. Unbelievably, we were confined to quarters for the rest of the trip.

· Splitting on the spouse ·

New York · I hear that Peter Holm, the Swedish ham who was once married to Joan Collins, is getting £250,000 for spilling the beans about the *Dynasty* star, which is certainly not as bad as what Judas did 1,954 years ago, but definitely along the same lines.

Vadim, Brigitte Bardot's ex, has also made a tidy sum by telling all about her, Jane Fonda and Catherine Deneuve, which does not really surprise me, as Vadim – a man I know quite well – has always been the type. He was Jane Fonda's guru for a long time, which doesn't explain why Fonda is as ghastly and phoney as she is, but does give her some kind of excuse.

And then there is Eddie Fisher, the man Elizabeth Taylor dumped a quarter of a century ago for Richard Burton. Fisher is a horrid little man who used to sing horrid little songs, but he came into his own, as they say in Hollywood, when he described in his book how he went to bed with Merle Oberon while her penultimate husband was in the next room. Although I like to think I have a pretty strong stomach, reading Fisher's pathetic prose did make me feel queasy, but what I really wanted to do was punch that indiscreet shit in the nose. (Which I like to imagine would have cost me a fortune, as Fisher's proboscis looks as phoney as his name.)

Which brings me back to Holm, and others of his ilk. One thing that has always amazed me about film stars of the fairer sex is the low quality of husbands they're more often than not saddled with. I guess it's because no self-respecting man will marry someone who spends all day rolling in the hay with another man while hundreds of randy extras are looking on. Whatever the reason, one thing is for sure. There is as much honour and dignity among Hollywood husbands as there is compassion in Tehran.

In Holm's case, not only is he not satisfied with 250 big ones, he also is demanding millions for having been married to Joan for less than a year. When I read of his demands, I must admit that I whistled that well-known aria from *South Pacific*, 'This nearly was mine, and then I thought better of it'.

But before any of you suspect that I'm about to join the sleaze brigade, here's a brief explanation: it was during a *Spectator* lunch nine years ago that Peregrine Worsthorne turned to me in mock admiration and announced that he was quite impressed to find out that I had once been Joan Collins's boyfriend. Now, there are few things I've not been accused of in my long and happy life, but spilling the beans about girls is not one of them. So I remember telling Perry not to believe everything he hears, and only half of what he sees (an old Turkish proverb) but he insisted. 'It's right there, in her book,' he told me.

And, sure enough, it was. As soon as the lunch was over I grabbed a taxi and headed for the closest bookshop downmarket enough to have *Past Imperfect* on sale. Her version of the time we spent together was pretty much the way I remember it, except for the fact that she had Nicky Hilton and me fighting in El Morocco over her, when in fact I had fought a man by the name of George de Witt; and another small detail involving an older gentleman.

Back in 1957 I used to get up every morning quite early, just before lunch, in fact, eat breakfast and then head for the tennis courts, where I would spend most of the afternoon. Joan would lunch with friends, or go shopping. One day a sudden downpour cancelled the tennis early, and I headed back to the hotel earlier than usual. While entering I noticed Joan having lunch in the grill with ... my father. I was surprised because I had no idea they knew each other, but appreciative of the fact that he would take the time to keep her company, I also noticed she was wearing a diamond pin in the shape of an anchor.

In her book, the older man was never named, therefore I won't name him either. But because it was so long ago, I might give you a hint. There are more women wearing jewels with a maritime theme around Athens than there are free-loaders at Aspinall's. All this came back to me when last in London I read an article that asked whether Joan must sometimes wonder who is left to kiss and tell. Not to worry, Joanie, this is as far as I'll ever go.

· Getting to like Jimmy ·

New York · Last week, while dining with the 39th President of the United States, Evelyn Waugh suddenly came to mind. If memory serves, he was once observed standing near the entrance of White's club, speaking to no one and staring at nothing in particular. When asked by fellow members if anything was wrong, Waugh shook his head and said he wished to be alone because he was a terrible shit, and a man who deserved no friends. Or something to that effect.

Given the fact that I am not half as nasty as Waugh was, I was not about to leave the table and stand by the hallway with a blank look of contrition on my face. Nor could I do a *mea culpa* in front of a lot of vastly overpaid American television media stars. So I did the next best thing and got blind drunk. So drunk, mind you, that I was the last to leave the dinner party after having trapped the poor peanut farmer in a corner and having explained to him at length why democracy was a biological contradiction.

Needless to say, I felt as lousy as I did because of the horrible things I've written and said about Jimmy Carter in the past. As it turns out, he was as nice and decent a man as he was an incompetent President. When I recounted how badly I felt to Pat Buckley, Bill's wife, she assured me that as a Christian I should not feel guilty. 'You hated the politician but liked the man,' was the way she put it. Amen, said I.

The dinner itself was excellent, and more fun than usual because the big shots I was sitting with ordered only Perrier water. Which meant I emptied all their glasses and talked non-stop about how ghastly television is in general, and American television in particular. I was seated in between Miss Diane Sawyer, a beautiful TV person, as they say nowadays, and Miss Helen Gurley Brown, of *Cosmopolitan* magazine fame. Miss Brown and I got along extremely well because she is old-fashioned, or at least she pretends to be old-fashioned when dining next to a male chauvinist who is proud of being a pig.

After dinner all the big shots headed for home, and that is when I trapped the poor ex-President. My argument was that he should not have felt sad once he was rejected by the public because had he done a good job, the populace was bound to resent him. (The ancient Greeks used to exile Aristides because he was never wrong.) Had he done a lousy job, he should have been happy to be replaced. I also proposed a plan of mine that guarantees everyone a vote, but some more than others, i.e., if a crack-dealer in Harlem has one vote, I, for example, have 25, and someone like General Patton 100, and so on. Jimmy, as I shall call him from now on, called it an interesting philosophical argument, but did not agree. After that I don't remember too much except that my hostess, Alice Mason, apparently escorted me out of her flat in order to make sure Carter would digest his dinner.

Jimmy Carter is as decent a man as it's possible to be – for a politician, anyway – but he was obviously so insecure that he projected his *malaise* on to society. And speaking of society, the next evening I participated in a discussion on social climbing at the New School's auditorium, a discussion that was chaired by my old friend Michael Thomas, the novelist and curmudgeon. The place was full and for once I was in good form as there were a few bright young things in the audience and I was eager to make a good impression.

My thesis, explained to me by my guru Professor Ernest van den Haag, went something like this. A snob is a person not born into the nobility who aspires to be with people he perceives to be his superiors. As today's New York society comprises such people as Gutfreund, Steinberg, Ertegun and Zipkin, there is no need to want to climb. I seem to have got my point across, because when the two hours were up I was literally mobbed by hysterical women trying to rip my clothes off. They only managed to get my cuff-links and part of my tie before the police hustled me away. But at last I have realized why rock stars hate women as much as they do. For one brief moment I was actually frightened.

This week, of course, is the one to end all weeks. First Sir James's blast at Cliveden, and then my cousin's wedding to Tracy Ward. Harry Worcester is a book reviewer, a rock star, a real-estate magnate, a sportsman of renown, and the older brother of Lord John Somerset, the protégé of Nile Rogers, a man who is to rock music what Marshal Ney was to the cavalry charge. It should be an interesting combination of people, and an even more interesting evening.

· Fall of the usher ·

I still haven't figured out whether the choice of the date for the great party Sir James Goldsmith gave on election night was fortuitous or not. What I do know for sure is that Jimmy's choice of Cliveden for the dance certainly was not. The house was built by a Duke of Buckingham, I believe – a name that is not synonymous with political moderation in English history. What is also certain is that the quality and amount of food and drink offered by Sir James would not be considered moderate even by ... Farouk, had the last Egyptian king and sybarite been around and lucky enough to be invited. There were more magnums of pink champagne than there are pinkoes in the BBC, and more orchestras playing non-stop jazz and golden oldies than there were serious candidates to be elected Prime Minister that night.

The only surprise was the number of hacks that were present. The first man I encountered upon entering the panelled great hall was none other than Nigel Dempster, followed in quick succession by Peregrine Worsthorne, Paul Johnson, Frank Johnson, John O'Sullivan, John Gross, and Lord Weidenfeld, who may be known as a publisher by the great British and American public, but who I suspect must be a journalist at heart. (Incidentally, Lord W. and I kissed and made up, which proves that if an Austrian epicure is given enough good food, music, and female company, he can forget and forgive anything and anyone.)

Ironically, the evening began on a sad note for me. I was seated between Bryan Ferry's wife Lucy and Cosima Fry, when the subject of age came up. Although married to one of the kindest men I know, Lucy must be the cruellest of women because she pointed out that by the year 2000 she would just about be 40 years of age. It sounded simply dreadful, and it depressed me to such an extent I began drinking in the manner I've been accustomed to when dining with ex-Presidents of the good old US of A. Mind you, even if Lucy had not been cruel, I needed a drink that night almost as badly as Khomeini needs to shoot people every day. I had arrived from New York the night before and gone straight to Aspinall's for Lord

Worcester's stag party. Although jet-lagged and tired, I did manage to give a speech that people present told me later was on a par with the best my ancestor Demosthenes ever gave, one that had 22 men open-mouthed and some even holding back tears. After that there was some successful gambling, followed by drinks at Annabel's, and then it was dawn and yet another night had slipped by without rest for the weary little Greek boy.

So, by the time I began circulating among the perambulating ghosts of Cliveden I was rather relaxed, and I reminisced with some political veterans of the early Sixties about the Cliveden swimming pool, the great gardens, even the fact that Sebastian Taylor had been invited for a change. There were celebrities galore, as well as tycoons and half of the aristocracy, but it was the amount of beautiful young girls present that made the greatest impression on me.

Needless to say, I was once again the last man to leave, and was driven home by a friend who took two hours to locate London, a mere 20 miles away. By then it was midday on Friday and it was time to start getting ready for the wedding of the year that was taking place the next day in Oxfordshire. Harry Worcester had very kindly asked me to be an usher, probably the worst decision he's ever bound to make in his life. I am not exactly an expert in things English in general, and English weddings in particular, so it would be an understatement of sorts if I said that I did not make a success of it. In fact, I was promptly told that I was useless and advised to sit down as soon as I had placed Bill Lovelady, the groom's fellow musician in the rock group The Business Connection, in the seat which the mother of the bride should have occupied. Which may have been a good thing after all. Because I did stand up for the next 18 hours, while attending the best dance for people who like Zulu music (the kind that keeps men and women apart while dancing) that I ever have and probably ever will.

Even the royals thought so, because when I looked around to see someone I could bore while others danced away, the only person I recognized was the heir to the throne and his brother. After we were hustled out around nine in the morning, we continued in a terrific mood back at the hotel most of us were staying in, but then I remembered there was a tennis match to be played the next day, something I will recount for you next week if the liver transplant I am having on Thursday is successful.

· Cash and carry ·

On the first rained-out Monday of the Wimbledon fortnight, I went to the Vanderbilt tennis club for a practice session indoors. While I waited for a court I watched in amazement as last Sunday's Wimbledon champ threw his racket against the wall, swore loudly and often, and behaved in a manner that McEnroe would approve of.

Later, in the locker room, I heard him moaning about his sore back while he lay flat out on the floor in obvious agony. In fact, I remember one of his flunkeys telling him to keep it quiet, as members crowded round. That evening, while dining at Aspinall's, I took Aspers aside and told him that there was absolutely no way Cash could ever get through a gruelling tournament like Wimbledon, and he should bet accordingly. Aspers, who plays tennis the way his gorillas play the harpsichord, argued with me, insisting that Cash had the kind of game that wins on grass. My suggestion was that Aspers stick to primates, which he knows all about, and leave the tennis to experts like myself.

Well, as some of you may have heard, Cash did get through, a fact I have not been allowed to forget by the Aspinall family in general, and Damian Aspinall in particular. (Damian switched his bet after my advice, and wagered on Nystrom as a dark horse.) I guess it just goes to show how little the Greeks know about tennis. What we do know about is phoney remains of the Colossus of Rhodes, and even phonier claims about Elgin Marbles.

Mind you, it's not the first time I've got it wrong where tennis is concerned. For five straight years I wagered Johnny Gold that Borg could not win Wimbledon, the years being 1976 to 1980. My most stupid bet was against Lew Hoad winning in 1957. I was travelling with Mervyn Rose, who had beaten Lew in five long sets in Rome six weeks earlier, and Rose convinced me that he would beat Hoad in the quarters at Wimbledon. As soon as I landed in England I began placing bets on Rose. Hoadie murdered him, as he did Ashley Cooper in the final.

One year later was my worst disaster where betting is concerned. I was playing the Volpi Cup in Venice, and getting the grand sum of

$50 plus expenses for the week. Throughout the spring and summer tournaments we had a poker game going. The players were Nicola Pietrangeli, the great Italian champ, Pancho Contreras, a good Mexican player, Beppe Merlo, known the world over for his loose-stringed racket and two-handed strokes, and a Yugoslav by the name of Plecevich. And yours truly. Players back then had the financial

freedom of Jeffrey Bernard, thus I managed to keep my head above water by betting recklessly and bluffing a lot. Plecevich was the poorer, and owed everyone money. In fact, his game was suffering as a result.

On a Thursday night, before the quarters, Nicola proposed we play without limit in order for the losers to have a chance to catch up, as the tour was breaking up, with some of us going on to Beirut and Istanbul, and others on to the grass court tournaments in the States. I agreed with alacrity. During a difficult hand I ended up with four tens and bet $10,000 hoping the rest would think I was bluffing and see me. Everyone dropped out except for Plecevich, who sat with his eyes closed, twitching and murmuring strange Croatian prayers. I did not want his money and asked him to drop out. Just as Pietrangeli began to complain that I had ruined the game with my wild wagers, Plecevich screamed, 'Look.'

I reluctantly showed him my four tens and was about to tell him that he did not have to pay when his trembling hands turned over four jacks. Contreras almost fainted, Merlo whistled, Nicola apologized to me, and Plecevich got down on his knees and prayed. He never played another tournament. Ten big ones back then, and in Yugoslavia to boot, was a small fortune, and I later heard that Plecevich built a house and started a business with my four tens.

I thought of all this last week when I ran into my old buddy Neale Fraser, the only man who won Wimbledon without a backhand. He was with Benson, and had dropped a lot racing. Not to worry, said Neale, I've got Cash at 16 to one. And took the time to explain to me why Cash would produce cash. Being Greek and a know-it-all, I told him that a man who goes bananas during a practice session can never get through Wimbledon. Next time I swear I'll stick to picking olives instead of Wimbledon winners.

· Youthful pleasures ·

Venice · The last time I visited the most enchanting city in the world was 20 years ago, for the ultimate ball the old Contessa Volpi was to give. By an ironic twist, both my future ex-wives were with me. I was then married to Christina, a child bride if ever there was one, but I already had my eye on a 20-year-old by the name of Alexandra. The ball was a great success, marred somewhat by the disappearance of a famous diamond necklace off the wrinkled neck of a rich *grande dame*. The police were called in and the usual suspects were searched – I was not among them – but the diamonds were never found. Perhaps it was an indication of things to come, because soon after the rich closed down their *palazzos* and surrounded themselves with minders rather than sycophants.

What I remember best about my last visit to Venice was a drink I had with Philippe Erlanger, the noted French historian and Napoleonic expert. Erlanger invited me to drinks at the Café Florien, and we spoke about the self-styled emperor some consider to be the first modern man. I cannot truly say that I learned a lot because the wise professor had a roving eye, but even this could not stop me from noticing how delightful Florien was.

Last Sunday I was back in Venice for the third time in 30 years, this time with only one ex-wife, my two children, and Professor van den Haag, a man also known to have a roving eye but for the fair sex only. Sitting once again in the Café Florien listening to its orchestra playing old romantic tunes, while drinking iced Tom Collinses and watching the old gas lamps flicker alight, brought back the memories of an irresponsible youth, and they were all pleasant ones. The city is so unique, it's almost impossible to feel sad, unless of course one is von Aschenbach and has it in for someone under age.

We stayed at the Cipriani for one night and two days, which at the present rate of exchange for the dollar comes to roughly the same amount won by Jeffrey Archer in his libel case against the smut merchants. The first night we dined at Harry's Dolci, in the Giudecca, a far better restaurant than Harry's Bar, if only for the lack of tourists. The next day we lunched at yet another Cipriani establishment in Torcello.

While Alexandra and I were taking in some culture under the expert instruction of our friend Ernest Van Den Haag, my two children and their nanny managed to spoil it all by hiring a taxi and cruising non-stop around the Venetian archipelago. I say they spoiled it all because taxis in Venice are not exactly like those in, say, Calcutta. By the time the brats had had enough cruising I was stuck with a bill of almost a million lire, and there was hell to pay. Literally.

But even the rapacious taxis of Venice did not spoil my mood. First there was the wonderful train back to Florence, air-conditioned, three-quarters empty, and on time. Then, of course, there was the good news that Aziz Kurtha and his kind had got their come-uppance, to add to my pleasure. Last was the fact that I've decided to buy a farmhouse in Tuscany, one that I shall put at the disposal of Mary and Jeffrey Archer, needless to say, although I suspect the Archers need Taki's house as much as England needs Kurtha the filth-pedlar.

Yes, it's been the most pleasurable of weeks and upon my return to Cetinale the best and most pleasant surprise of all was an 18-year-old by the name of Sophia Creswell, who might just become the third Mrs Taki. If you don't hear from me next week, look for me in the bottom of the well high above Lord Lambton's house. The suspects are Alexandra and Sophia's grandmother.

· Some like it hot ·

Athens · This is the first time in the ten years I have been writing on high life from the cradle of selective democracy that I have some good news to report. Artwise. Looking around me, it is obvious to even as biased a person as myself that the Athenians of the Papandreou period have finally caught up with those black and Hispanic draughtsmen New York sociologists refer to as graffiti or subway artists.

As there is no underground in the birthplace of oligarchy, the descendants of Apelles practise their art on every available building, dwelling, and statue of the ancient city. Needless to say, there are no greens or parks either, only cement, which helps art flourish as never before. At least not since the Golden Age of Pericles. In fact, so much so one feels that the only difference between being above ground in Athens or below ground in New York is the muggers. There are no muggers in the streets of Athens because they're all in the ministries and in parliament.

This week, while the temperature soars to numbers which would make the devil himself demand an air-conditioner, the muggers are all busy at work in their cool offices. The pro-government newspapers and the government-controlled radio and television (the telephones are government-controlled too, otherwise I would phone this story in) are busy extolling the work habits of the muggers, but I know better. Air-conditioners have been known to break down in private houses, but never in ministries.

In the meantime, the minister of health, a clown by the name of Mangakis, which literally translated means a little rascal, went on television and proudly announced that the armed forces were on alert to combat the next heat wave, and reassured the populace that there would be fewer deaths this time around. The result was that one and a half million Athenians fled the city in panic. Mangakis, however, proved himself right. Very few died of the heat, but a hell of a lot died in car accidents during the exodus.

Mangakis, incidentally, is an old buddy of mine. I was once asked to round up a few dissidents just after the fall of the colonels for a

William F. Buckley television show regarding Greece, and I thought the little rascal might make a good guest. Being a gentleman of the old school, I did not challenge him when he assured me his English was better than the Queen's. Once the cameras began rolling, I began to wonder which queen he had in mind. It must have been Cleopatra because most dogs I know understand more English than he did.

But never mind. Why complain about the little rascal's English, when his Greek ain't so good either? When some brave soul said he should resign following the deaths of so many poor and elderly, the minister of 'health' answered that he didn't understand what the brave soul meant.

I guess being elderly is not what it used to be in the birthplace of Melina Mercouri. Once the Papandreou regime got rid of the local oldies, they turned their attention to the foreign ones. The British granny who failed to serve cucumber or tomatoes, but served chilli sauce instead, and was thrown into prison for it, is the first example that comes to mind. Then there was an old lady from Czechoslovakia who drove her new Mercedes to Greece (she sold her house after her husband's death and bought a diesel Mercedes 200) and had it confiscated due to an error of the customs authorities which listed the car as illegally imported. When the error was traced the car had already been sold in auction at way below its market price and the buyer refused to return it. Oh yes, I forgot to mention who the buyer was: Yannis Papadopoulos, an MP for the Papandreou clique, and former minister for northern Greece.

Members of parliament have priority when confiscated cars are sold in auction, but the fact that their favourite pastime is to gawk at Audis and BMWs at border crossings I am sure is only paranoia on my part. I guess I'm a suspicious soul, but that's what happens when one is a third-rate writer living in the Golden Age of Andreas.

· Into my sixth decade ·

Athens · George Will is the very talented American writer who takes himself almost as seriously as *Guardian* women take themselves. When Will became 40 he wrote a column under the heading, 'On turning 40'. It was a very good column, and I expect old George will write one on becoming 50, 55, 60, 70, 71, 72, and so on.

Needless to say, I haven't got Will's talent for introspection, or for offering *bons mots* about the ageing of my fellow man, so I will simply tell you that the best thing about becoming 50 was the party I threw for myself last week. As more than two million neo-Hellenes had left for the countryside, I decided to have my party where the modern Greeks were least likely to be, and that was in the capital. Xenou, to be precise.

Xenou is a taverna I have often written about in the *Spectator*'s pages, so I will only mention the fact that it's located in Plaka, the old part of the city, and it's frequented by writers more than tourists. On the night of my birthday, however, there were only gays, and foreign gays, to boot. Now, as everyone who knows me knows, I don't mind gays as long as they don't try to proselytize my children to their way of life. For some strange reason, on this particular night there wasn't a single proselytizer among them, and when Mr Xenos and all his waiters came out into the garden to serenade me, every limp wrist in the place joined in. It was a touching scene, and it became even touchier when, in order to make the foreigners feel at home, I stood up and announced to the gays that I, too, was as queer as they were.

This, needless to say, did not go down well with the mother of my children, my karate team, the few girls I've promised marriage to, and – most important of all – the waiters of Xenou. Nevertheless, the retsina flowed like the Arno did when it overflowed in 1966, and by the time we closed the place it was clear to all of us that after three generations Xenou would soon turn into a gay bar.

The good thing about Athens without Athenians is that when I rang the latest 'in' place down by the sea and asked them to wait for us, they were only too happy to comply with our wishes. That is where my old friend Leonidas Goulandris joined me. Leonidas went to my old school, but for some strange reason he now works for the city's female census board. Or at least that is the impression he gives, because he literally knows every single female in town. The reason he had not joined me earlier was a new arrival from the States, one that Leonidas, always conscientious and working overtime, was adding to his lists.

Now I cannot think back and find among the many happy birthdays I've had a happier one than this one. It seems every good friend I have in Athens – and I've got lots – had the same idea, and had stayed behind. Also, Leonidas had come up with enough young and beautiful girls to make a London dance look like Xenou's on my birthday. Well, after the sun began making people take their clothes off for comfort, the party went on. My old friend Zographos, on the wagon for months, broke his vows and downed bottle after bottle. George Demetriades, a very old friend who once produced a plastic automobile – and had it half-eaten by a mule Zographos and I sneaked into his workroom – decided to forgive us, and joined in the celebration of my maturity.

When the mother of my children kissed me goodnight, I took a large party back to the Caravel hotel, of which I am president, and invited the ladies of the night as they were emerging from their clients' rooms to join us. Then we all dressed like Arabs and waited for the real McCoy to come down for lunch in order to discuss the problems of the Gulf, but that is when saner heads prevailed by reminding me that it was no use alienating the few customers we had, and we reluctantly bade each other goodnight.

The trouble with such juvenile shenanigans is that when one writes about them they sound just plain stupid. Well, they were anything but, as far as I'm concerned. In fact, I have decided now that I've crossed the Rubicon of 50 to really start to enjoy myself. As Oscar Wilde could have said, after all, it is only superficial people who act seriously at parties. And the only thing I felt serious about that night was a girl called Marina.

Well, George Will may be appalled at this description of turning 50, but he's too old to judge. I only wish Jeff had come down.

· Captains courageous ·

Spetsai · Bouboulina is a Greek heroine of our war of independence against the Ottoman Empire. She was born in an Istanbul jail while her mother was visiting her father, who had been imprisoned by the Turks for having followed Admiral Orlof when the Russian prince made his premature move against the Sultan.

By a strange coincidence, Bouboulina's mother married a sea captain by the name of Orlof after her husband died in jail. The sea captain was a Greek from Spetsai, and there are still a lot of Orlofs living on the island at present. By an even stranger quirk of fate, Bouboulina herself was killed – some say murdered – by her half-brother, Lazaros Orlof, after an argument over family matters. Before her death, however, she had spent her vast fortune (sea captains back then were richer than ship-owners were ten years ago) in building ships to fight against the Ottomans, ships that she personally captained, incidentally.

Her flagship was the *Agamemnon*, a boat that ran circles round the Turkish fleet in the Peloponnese, and from which she led many successful attacks against the Sultan's sailors. She retired almost penniless to Spetsai in 1825, and died three months later. There are a few streets named after her in Greece today, and a rather ugly statue of her off the main square in Spetsai, but otherwise her descendants have not exactly been taken care of by the state in the style in which it cares for its politicians and civil servants.

Bouboulina was a member of the 'Filiki Etereia', a group of Greeks living outside occupied Hellas who financed the war of independence. So was an ancestor of mine, and I guess this is why in Spetsai last weekend I took the side of an Orlof against a bunch of ship-owners.

Spetsai is located some 60-odd miles south of Athens, a distance I can cover in less than two hours on my old man's gin palace, which can cruise at 35 knots. Last week I packed the boat with friends and headed down to visit my English buddies, some of whom own houses on the island. Spetsai and its environs attract the best as well as the ghastliest of foreigners. There are people like the Russells, the Trees and the Deons, and then there are some people whom even the gutter wouldn't accept. Needless to say, I visited the former, namely Alexander Russell and his bride of one year, Libby Manners.

The only trouble with Alexander is that he's too generous. (He's half Greek, and that's where the generosity comes from.) He plied me with so much drink that by the time I left his house my sailors had to help me stand upright. Worse, the boat was anchored in the old harbour, a stone's throw from a nightclub called Figaro. Leonidas Goulandris, a man who could impoverish Paul Getty were the latter a friend of his, insisted we go for one last one. So off we went to the Figaro, a rather expensive decision as it turned out.

As I don't remember most of the details, I will not bore you with them, but I do recall receiving a bill of about £900 for three bottles of whisky. Being too drunk to protest, I simply remained in my seat while some of my friends made vague signs of displeasure. Finally I told the management to come round to the boat in the morning to collect their blood money.

The waiter who had presented me with the bill was a local boy by the name of Orlof. He is of the family I mentioned previously. The next day he cheerfully informed us that he had made a mistake, and presented me with a normal bill. Soon after some vulgarians arrived and asked me to tell the police about the bill of the night before. I asked them why, and they told me that they had been overcharged and were trying to recover their loot. That is when I became Hamlet. My ambivalence, however, did not go over big with the vulgarians. Just come and tell the truth, they wailed. So I did. I testified that I had not been overcharged, and that Orlof had more integrity than all his accusers put together. End of case.

So, now I've once again made more friends among the parvenus in Spetsai, and once again I learned the difference between lying and withholding the truth. I certainly didn't commit the former, and anyone related to Bouboulina certainly deserved the latter. If Greece were a proper country, the parvenus would be wearing the white jackets, not Orlof.

· Got any good ... ·

Athens · They say that nothing is capable of raising one's posthumous status more than the way one faces those last few moments before meeting what W. C. Fields called the fellow in the bright nightgown. Oscar Wilde was witty to the bitter end, as was Voltaire. (Do you renounce the devil? Certainly not. This is no time to make new enemies.) John Barrymore hammed it up. Just as the nurse adjusted the sheets on his bed, he winked and said, 'OK, hop in!' He then died. America's platinum king, Charlie Engelhard, was no Voltaire. His last words were, 'Bring me a Coke.'

The greatest Greek writer since Aristophanes did no better than old Charlie upon reaching Hades' goal line – 'Bloody jellyfish,' would have been my last two words had not the Almighty made sure to pump that extra cubic centimetre of blood through my coronary artery. A posthumous downer if ever there was one.

But not to worry. As soon as I get hold of Jeff ('Out of Africa') Bernard, I promise to come up with some better lines. Jeff, as we all know, has been holding dress rehearsals for years, and gossip has it that his exit line will be superior to those of Wilde, Voltaire, and Barrymore put together. After all, practice makes perfect, and no one has practised harder than old Jeff.

How did I manage to be in the running for corny old exit lines? Easy. An hour and a half of violent karate training, followed by an all-nighter with a very sweet brown belt, two packets of Papastratos without filter, one bottle of whisky and half a bottle of brandy, and presto, the stage was set. On Saturday morning my father took a look at me and ordered me on board his boat. He then took off for Spetsai. Once there I lunched and decided to go for a swim, having noticed some English friends nearby. While swimming back, I suddenly felt something bite me hard on the chest. For one moment I took it to be a sand shark and began to thrash around. Then I realized it must be a school of jellyfish, so I swam back as fast as I could in order to get away from them. Once on board, however, I could find nothing on my chest to indicate a bite, although it continued to hurt quite a lot. I figured it must have been a female jellyfish, and left it at that.

The pain did not go away, however, and that evening I decided to stay on board. Throughout the night I tossed and turned, unable to sleep, while the chest pains got worse. The captain, who I am now informed used to be a butcher before taking to sea, assured me I had nothing to worry about. He went so far as to say the jellyfish came from Turkey, and that Turkish jellyfish were known to bring on a high fever. In the morning, my daddy took a second look, and sped back to Athens. There the family doctor diagnosed a massive heart attack and ordered me straight to hospital.

Now, as everyone who has read Jeff's accounts of his various hospital stays knows, only a fool would try and emulate his descriptions. Suffice it to say that I was in a private room, and felt too ill to pick up the gallows humour that hospital wards are known for. The best I can do is repeat the joke of an elderly cancer patient who sat and chain-smoked outside my room: 'What is 14 inches long and hangs down to the knees of Andreas Papandreou?' The answer is his necktie, and if I heard it once I swear I heard it one hundred times in the week I was in there.

Needless to say, my father cancelled his cruise with his latest girlfriend (she's Miss Greece, and 30 years younger than I am) and spent his time at my bedside. In fact, he felt so sorry for me, he suddenly announced he was rewriting his will and leaving everything to me, not the smartest of moves in case of my snuffing it, unless he wishes to pay Papandreou twice. My mother, more practical, prayed non-stop.

Yes, there is nothing like a little old heart attack to make one Mr Popular overnight. Even my wife Alexandra has come around and forgiven me everything, not to mention my older brother. In the meantime, I'm out of hospital and resting before flying to London in the near future. I am reading *Germinal*, by Joe Biden, and *Across the River and into the Trees*, by Teddy Kennedy, and it helps pass the time. I am also picking up some good exit lines.

· Windy city wind-bag ·

Chicago · The Oprah Winfrey show is the most popular daytime television show in the good old USA, which means it is watched by tens of millions of people who – I assume – are both illiterate as well as terribly concerned with such weighty matters as day-care centres for one-armed Navajo Indian single mothers.

The reason Oprah is a favourite of mine is simple. Until she came along, Phil Donahue, the dumbest man I have ever had the bad luck to cross swords with, was king of daytime TV. No longer. Last week I flew to Chicago and appeared on Oprah's show for the second time in three years, the subject being older men who prefer younger women. My friend Chuck Pfeiffer and I were lucky to get out of the studio alive and sound of limb.

But before I give you the gory details, a brief résumé of my American television career is in order. It all began long ago when I wrote an anti-feminist tract in the *American Spectator* entitled 'American Women are Lousy Lovers'. Needless to say, it had nothing whatsoever to do with the sexual act, but simply poked fun at today's feminists who see everything in terms of conquest. Just as needless to say, television producers were bound to jump at the title without ever bothering to read the contents.

Sure enough, the Donahue show flew me first class all the way from Athens to Chicago, where I managed a draw with his female audience, but showed him up as the ignoramus and wimp that he is. Three months later I went on to the Oprah show, and that turned out to be great fun. Oprah is intelligent, and when I told her my ideal woman was the proverbial whore in the bedroom, cook in the kitchen, and lady in the drawing-room, she and some other black girls in the audience began cheering.

Last week, yet again, only three members of the black race sided with Pfeiffer and myself. When Oprah asked Chuck and me why we preferred younger women, I chickened out and said that younger women were more likely to put up with silly pursuits such as night-clubbing and heavy drinking, whereas older women, being more mature, would never put up with it.

The mostly female audience seemed to like that, but then Captain Pfeiffer got into action, and we were suddenly rather unpopular. 'Only a blind man would prefer an older woman,' bellowed the good captain, and the hissing drowned out the rest of his philippic. To make matters worse, three black men stood up and agreed with us, and managed to get us into trouble through association by explaining

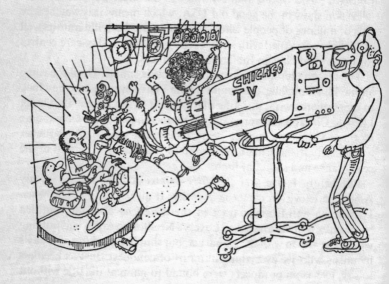

that their preference for younger women was based on older women ... smelling bad.

While dodging rotten vegetables I tried my best to recover some ground by evoking the Don Giovanni syndrome, of men thinking they'll find happiness through variety, but it was too late. We were good-naturedly booed off the stage, and probably off television for ever. Which was the first good news of the day.

But more was still to come. Christopher Gilmour is a good friend of mine, an Englishman who lives and works in what is definitely the most beautiful, cleanest and best-run big city in America. Christopher immediately planned the rest of our day – and night – and it made all the booing worthwhile. Christopher knows the right spots in Chicago as well as, say, Liz Taylor knows the good hairdressers of this world. I don't think I've met a nicer bunch of people than his friends, or had a better time since Tuscany.

The three nightclubs he took us to make anything Noo York – with the exception of Nell's – has to offer seem like a Beirut dive. Chicago itself is a warm and hospitable city, with the beautiful modern buildings fitting in comfortably with the old, a romantic modernism of sorts. Plus the trains run on time. But it was the realization that people are truly nice the moment one leaves the ghastly Big Bagel that made the trip worthwhile, something I had always suspected. America without New York and Los Angeles would be a far greater country than it already is.

· Getting into trouble ·

Palm Beach · Palm Beach is a pristine, immaculate resort north of Miami, a place full of palm trees, great mansions by the sea, and multi-millionaires, where law and order reign supreme, and where socialists are as rare as socialites in Qum.

It is the most famous watering-place in America, and deservedly so. It reeks of money and comfort, a toy town for the very rich, a village where one can buy a Mercedes or a diamond but cannot have one's shirt laundered.

Last week I was the second poorest visitor in Palm Beach, and I say second, because a broken-down English friend of mine by the name of Nick Simunek was also there. But first, more about the place.

I first visited it as a schoolboy. My parents brought me down for the Christmas break and I immediately got into trouble. It was in 1954, and the liquor laws permitted a 17-year-old to drink. On New Year's Eve I got totally sloshed, and after my parents went to bed, I raced my then new best friend, Sean Flynn, all over the Everglades Club golf course. Sean had a motorcycle, and I had a Ford Thunderbird. He got the best of me, which was a blessing in disguise, as it turned out.

Early the next morning two extremely stern-looking state troopers trooped into my room in the Breakers Hotel, roused me out of bed and took me down to the police station. Once there I was charged with the destruction of private property, namely four greens of the Everglades golf club. Sean Flynn, son of Errol, was also there, looking sheepish and contrite. The damage was estimated at $30,000, which in today's climate could be closer to $200,000. It was $29,990 more than Sean and I had between us.

Needless to say, his mother, Lily Damita, an old resident of Palm Beach, and my old man came to the rescue. The club was insured and after some extremely stern warnings we were allowed to go home. The fact that witnesses had testified that I was a follower, not the leader, helped. Sean was put on probation, and I was told to stay away for 50 years or so. But I was back two years later, and Sean and I basked in the notoriety our idiotic prank had brought us. (Sean and I remained friends until his disappearance in the Cambodian jungle in 1970.)

Like every other resort, Palm Beach was smaller and friendlier during the Fifties and early Sixties. I tried to go there at every opportunity, spending my days playing tennis at the Bath and Tennis Club, my nights at the Taboo and Alibi. I made many friends. Then people like Donald Trump, the real-estate developer, invaded West Palm Beach, and began putting up high-rise buildings. The *nouveaux riches* came down with a vengeance, and it was time for Palm Beach clubs to barricade themselves.

Last week I arrived at the Bath and Tennis and was made to wait at the entrance while they searched for my host. Security is now very strict, almost as strict as the rules that forbid any ethnic or religious minorities to enter the club. During lunch Chuck Pfeiffer and I made the mistake of drinking one bloody mary too many and becoming obstreperous. Our host, a very old friend, became uneasy. 'Take it easy,' he kept repeating. 'You'll get me thrown out.' Of course, we did nothing of the sort, but then Nick Simunek may have. Simunek is a terrible drunk, but with a terrific sense of humour. He came into the club feeling no pain and in the company of the raunchiest girl this side of Beirut. Being kind-hearted, we tried to see her good side. 'She looks awfully rich,' I yelled to him. 'Rich? You should see her tits,' he shouted back across an appalled Wasp dining-room.

I guess all good things have an end, and my Bath and Tennis days ended with Nick's crude but rather poignant remark. Oh, well, there is always Trump Plaza across the bridge.

1988

· Piste off ·

I was warned by some of the most important people I know that London would be quiet this time of year. What they didn't tell me was how quiet. Annabel's this week resembled an anti-Khomeini pep rally in downtown Tehran, and things got so bad at Tramps that Johnny Gold waived the ban on the English for the duration.

Worse, my mantelpiece is as bare as Charles Benson's bank balance, which indicates that my social life is about to follow the stock market in 1988. Mind you, I did have a pleasant surprise when Lady Edward Somerset rang to invite me to Badminton for the weekend, which proves, I guess, that even the Dukes around this town are pushed for company. The great Oscar once said that to be popular one has to be a mediocrity, but I ain't convinced.

What I am convinced of is that I'd be in Gstaad, rather than posing as a hermit in SW3, had the good Lord dropped some white stuff over the Alps. The last time the Bernese Oberland resembled El Alamein was back in 1964, and I spent the whole month of January walking up the Wassengrat with Irwin Shaw, and playing tennis with my friend Philippe Washer. In fact, none of us missed the skiing, especially as the Palace gave us a discount which we paid with the then almighty 4.30 Swiss francs to the dollar.

Needless to say, such are the joys of Bakernomics, 24 years later it's almost cheaper to give a dinner for six at Mark's Club than to swing for a couple of pitta-bread sandwiches in the *buffet de la gare* of Saanen. But never mind. Money isn't everything, as my rich socialist friends tell me, especially when things are bound to get worse as far as the root of all socialist envy is concerned.

What I find far more disturbing is the Stalingrad-like siege imposed upon my favourite *station d'hiver* by my fellow countrymen. It seems that some of Premier Papandreou's nearest and dearest invaded Gstaad over the holidays and, worse, not content with sending postcards back to the Olive Republic, insisted on lunching at the Eagle Club, to boot. The Trojan horse turned out to be the daughter of Greece's richest man, which proves once and for ever that Virgil was right on.

I guess the only defence left to me is to once again run for president of the club, as I did exactly ten years ago when I came in second. For those of you who didn't read the *Spectator* ten years ago, the voting process begins by discreet canvassing the year before an election. Being the only member – along with my friend Zographos – who had been elected twice (we had been thrown out for brawling with an English civil servant), I thought it only fair to lead the club into the Eighties. So I approached my fellow Greeks and asked them to write in their vote with my name on it as a joke. Just before the general meeting was held, the retiring president took a look at the proxy votes and almost had a stroke. Only about 15 out of 300 members had voted, and I was leading 15-love.

Alas, the bores carried the day, and I came in second best out of two (285–15, to be exact). But like Gary Hart I am once again a candidate, convinced I am the man to lead the club into the Nineties, and like Gary I plan to run my campaign on the cheap, from Annabel's.

And speaking of changing the guard, Aspinall's now belongs to Peter de Savary, which means Princess Michael will be taking up punto-banco in the near future. I dropped in for a quick loss earlier this week, and the place looked like the Maginot Line the day after Guderian's armour had set the world's land speed record while crossing it. Everything was spick and span, as if nothing had changed, but the regulars looked awfully worried. Good habits – such as free booze and food – are very hard to break, and for the moment there is fear and loathing in Curzon Street. In fact, Charles Benson, a prudent man, has already lost two stone in anticipation.

· Writer's block ·

I've been a good boy all week, laying off the booze and staying away from Annabel's and Tramps, but the *Ballad of Pentonville Gaol* is doing a Schubert's Ninth on me. However much I torture my mind and body by waking up early, drinking beer rather than whisky and keeping company with pederasts and intellectuals, it now looks certain that the only prize I shall be winning this year is the coitus interruptus one. Since I've come to London, I've managed to put down as many words on paper as that moustachioed clown in Managua has instilled reforms.

But never mind. There are more important things in life than prison diaries, such as television programmes about ... books. In America, where people have the right priorities, the only book show is on cable television, in French, and it's shown on Channel J, the pornographic channel. It's called *Apostrophe*, and in New York it claims a wide audience of rapists, flashers and a myriad of wankers.

Over here, however, things are different. This week I appear on *Cover to Cover*, the BBC's book review programme chaired by Jill Neville, whose audience is slightly different from the one I mentioned above. On Tuesday, Professor Malcolm Bradbury, Michele Roberts, Tom Wolfe and I sat down and discussed Tom's great novel *The Bonfire of the Vanities*.

I first read *The Bonfire* late last year and thought it was the best book ever written about life in the Big Bagel. While leafing through it again, I came to the conclusion that Wolfe is as likely to win the Pulitzer Prize for literature as Kurt Waldheim is to become president of Israel. First of all, the novel reads as if one is on uppers, a cardinal sin as far as the prize-givers are concerned. Secondly, Wolfe is simply too honest and far too accurate about such unmentionable subjects as class warfare, liberal hypocrisy, black and Jewish greed and the motives of those who defend the underclasses of Noo Yawk. Telling it like it is might sound good, but it won't get a writer far with the American intelligentsia. At least not if the writer is male, white, heterosexual, and a political moderate. Oh, yes, I almost forgot, also without a record like mine.

Typically, the reviews of the book over here have been much better than over there. And I must commend the *Observer*'s reviewer who was the only one to spot the incredible *faux pas* of calling a knight's daughter a lady. Bravo; it proves to me that social status consciousness is alive and well among Tiny's minions. For a while I was worried, especially once they moved close to Harrods.

Although I never thought I'd say it in print, one can have a wonderful time at parties while staying off the booze in order to write. Last week I went to a party for Anne Somerset and drank water throughout. The results were quite startling. Not only do I remember everything people said, I also have total recall about what I did. The trouble is that nobody else does.

I had dined at Marianne Hinton's and driven to Elgin Marbles road with my friend Mark Getty. Once inside the house I spotted some literary heavyweights like Emma Soames and Geoffrey Wheatcroft and made a beeline for them in order to show off the new, improved Taki. Emma, who is the only editor-in-chief of a magazine that is bonkable, cut me dead. Something to do with the troubles in Cyprus back in 1959, I presume. Wheatcroft ditto. So I walked around the house trying to make friends with upper-crust people who eat food rather than throw it, but to no avail. I soon gave up and headed home, having learned a good lesson. Which is that staying sober at parties makes one as fascinating to the fair sex as Jesse Jackson is to the Ku Klux Klan.

Next week I fly to the Big Olive to try yet again to put Oscar Wilde to shame. Jeff, in the meantime, is taking book at the Coach and Horses that I'll never finish, and offering 50–1 odds.

· Call to arms ·

I remember it as if it were yesterday. Hundreds of Princeton University students demonstrating behind a giant sign that read: 'Nothing is worth dying for.' It was the day after President Reagan had decreed that all eligible young men should register for the draft. This was about five or six years ago.

Cut to a beautiful alpine valley surrounded by snowy mountains on a spring morning last week. The only sound is the laughter of the skiers and of gunfire. Bearded middle-aged men wearing combat uniforms and helmets and loaded down with automatic weapons and 40-pound sacks are moving slowly up the paths on both sides of the valley. The railway station is full of reserve troops on their way to refresher courses in civil defence. It is obvious, even to mindless, publicity-craving jet-setters, that this is Switzerland, and that gunfire and real war games are not unusual. Even in Gstaad.

Driving up the Saanen valley towards Schoenried last week, Bill Buckley pointed out that what would be unusual would be to encounter an anti-military demonstration. 'The Swiss have enjoyed 450 years of peace because they know there are some things worth dying for,' is the way I believe my friend Bill put it.

It is a tradition that dates back to the 13th century, in which Switzerland has never ceased to maintain a militia-type army for her defence. Military service, in fact, is a way of life over there, with every physically capable male citizen keeping his gun, ammo and bayonet at home. The crime rate is one of the lowest in the world, if not the lowest.

Now cut back to a few choice locations in the US and right here in Britain. We see ugly women blocking access to American air bases, hirsute professors picketing enlistment centres, drunken plagiarist senators denouncing military spending. No wonder the great Solzhenitsyn said there is absolutely no likelihood of nuclear war, for we are ready to throw in the towel at the sight of the first Soviet tank.

I thought of all these weighty subjects while whizzing down beautiful powder on my last day in God's country last week. Perhaps there is something perverse about skiing for pleasure while thousands of men are on military manoeuvres, but the soldiers I ran into did not seem to mind. They laughed and shouted whenever somebody took a fall, and went about their business. Which was, I assume, stock-piling the mountains in case of an emergency. Swiss ministry of defence officials estimate that in the event of total blockade present stocks, including local food production, would permit both military and civilians to survive for up to ... five, yes, five years. Special roads have been built for use as landing strips, while every bridge and tunnel can be mined and destroyed in a matter of minutes.

All this, needless to say, makes one feel not only safe, but confident of the future. Although there are those who complain non-stop about how dull the Swiss are, I ain't among them. What's so dull about people who want to remain free and their own masters? What is so interesting about a species such as the draft-age American generation that states unequivocally that nothing is worth dying for?

In a recent poll of the United States the baby-boomers were asked under what circumstances they would be willing to serve in the armed forces and go to war, and 40 per cent of them answered 'under no circumstances'. To add insult to injury, those very same people chose Robert Kennedy as their all-time hero along with Martin Luther King. It is enough to make any red-blooded man move to Switzerland, something I hope to do very soon. Just as soon as I make enough root of all envy to be able to afford it. One thing is for sure, however. If any of you out there are counting on Americans to help us in case of war, you had better start waiting for Godot instead. Better yet, the Swiss army.

· Improving with age ·

The vote on the affair was pretty much unanimous. This was the most smashing shindig in years, one worth raving about long after the last drunk is discovered sleeping it off somewhere in the grounds of the great Badminton House. I for one had such a wonderful time, and got so depressed when it was over at 8.30 a.m., that I swore to the people who were literally showing me the door that it was the last ball I'd ever attend. An oath which naturally I do not intend to keep, but gave in order to make my point. The fact is, though, that future parties are bound to suffer by comparison, so I plan to lie doggo for a while.

There was one guest – an academic I believe – who left early. He was heard to mutter something about being snubbed by Princess Michael of Kent, an obvious lie as the princess was dining with Taki of all people. (Plus a few others.) The irony is that the last time the Duke and Duchess of Beaufort gave a ball at Badminton back in 1973, give or take a year, it was also for their daughter Anne, but I didn't enjoy myself half as much. It's obvious that like a good wine, I'm improving as a ball-goer with age. I guess Proust was right when he said that verbalists, rather than doers, advance in the pecking order at parties, as back then I was a rather shy young man whom no one paid any attention to, while this time I noticed being noticed by some even while having a rest underneath the dining-room table.

The occasion for the ball was Anne Somerset's wedding to Matthew Carr, which took place in the small 17th-century church located rather conveniently in the courtyard of the house. And what a lovely wedding it was. The church is lined with memorial plaques of various Somerset family members, is light and airy and with wonderful acoustics. It was a brief and touching ceremony in intimate surroundings. Everything that grand weddings nowadays ain't. What I particularly like about Church of England weddings is that they're all business, i.e. they get on with the business of getting people hitched, unlike the Greek Orthodox ones which last as long as three hours.

Because of Anne's wedding I had the earliest start since Pentonville. My friend of 31 years, Mickey Suffolk, Earl of Suffolk and Berkshire to the rest of you Brits, had invited me to stay at Charlton Park, his family house since the days of another Elizabeth Regina. The last time I had stayed with Mickey he was a bachelor and we managed to get into some trouble when someone had the bright idea of raiding a nearby house and switching all the furniture around.

But before we began to move things around we ran into the master of the house furiously copulating with, of all people, his own wife. He wasn't best pleased to find five intruders in his bedroom – I remember Mickey was even commenting on the performance – and ushered us out by waving his shotgun towards us.

This time things were far more civilized. Linda Suffolk is as nice as she is hospitable, although I'm sure the Kents might think she's too hospitable once they realized who they were dining with. But everything was hunky-dory until ball time and then – needless to say – things began to blur at the edges. (Suffolk had served a white Château Margaux that Jeff Bernard would give up vodka for, and the red was just as good. The problem is that such wines tend to make one drink more, and, well, you know the rest.) But I do remember standing and talking to people like Jacob Rothschild (someone came up and commented rather rudely that one can tell a successful ball when people like Jacob speak to people like Taki), Ernst of Hanover, Peter Saunders (I once tried to buy his daughter from him but he refused), Jonathan Guinness, plus another ten or 15 of that species, the new editor of *Tatler*, the ex-*Sunday Telegraph* social columnist, my Tuscan host Lord Lambton, and the girl I've had an eye on for a long time, Sophia Murphy, who got so bored with my psychobabble she left almost as early as the academic.

And speaking of academics, the father of the groom, Sir Raymond Carr, was cornered by yours truly and people tell me the old boy will never be the same again. Apparently I wanted to know what the meaning of life is, but he understood that I was asking him for the definition of fore-play, so he answered, '30 minutes of begging'.

· If you knew Suzy ·

New York · The best newspaper in America, the *Wall Street Journal*, front-paged the story and relegated that egregious midget Michael (beware of Greeks wearing lifts) Dukakis where he belongs. ABC and CNN news led their broadcast with it. My live-in girlfriend Liz Smith has written two of her widely syndicated columns about it, and there are follow-up stories about the brouhaha in the Gannett chain of papers, the *Washington Post*, *Newsweek* and even the dull old *Big Bagel Times*.

Needless to say, I am talking about the greatest feud since Jerry Zipkin fought the tiny terror Truman Capote outside the Beverly Hills Hotel ten years or so ago. It is Aileen Mehle *vs* James Revson, and before any of you go running for your *Who's Who*, I'll explain:

Aileen Mehle is a gossip writer based in New York whose finest moment came when she flew to London to give evidence against the greatest Greek writer since Aristophanes. She writes under the pen name of Suzy, and her style has been described as sycophantic at best. Her forte is the very, very rich, the very, very old, and the very, very social. She fawns over them, and they in turn invite her to their parties. In fairness, Suzy is more of a propagandist for the rich than a gossip columnist, and also in fairness, she is a pro at what she does and she has been doing it for 30 or more years.

James Revson I do not know, although I know his brother and used to know his cousin the racing driver. His family owned Revlon before it was taken over by one of Suzy's chums, Ronald Perelman. Revson writes a gossip column for *Newsday*, a Long Island paper, and picked the fight with an exposé of Suzy under the heading 'Desperately seeking Suzy' in which he revealed that Suzy had reported about a dance that she never attended. Worse, she had named a lot of people as being present who were not, and to top it all off, he revealed that Suzy was sunning herself down south while pretending to be working up north.

Well, my dears, Suzy's response was as disproportionate as, say, that of the Greeks over the cuckolding of Menelaus. Here are a few of the choice names she called poor Revson in print: 'Dear Rat. Get lost. You can't leave town any more without the crock hitting the fan. This time the slime oozed from a jerk at *Newsday*, a know-nothing who has aspirations of writing a social column.' She then went on for over 2,000 words calling him, among other things, a liar, an ass, a snake and a nobody. And for good measure she sent out a warning to all the big shots in the Big Bagel that it was either she or he from now on. 'Do not invite me anywhere if you invite him. Just call it a boycott.'

Now, I am the last person to take the socialites of this town seriously, but even I was surprised how seriously the social ones take Suzy. Two of them, Alice Mason and Anne Slater – who ironically happen to be friends of mine – went on record as saying they would rather die than ever speak to Revson again. Jerry Zipkin also heaped abuse on Revson while calling Suzy the greatest woman since Joan of Arc. It looked as if Suzy had wiped the floor with poor James until, well, for lack of a better word, nemesis reared up in the form of Suzy's opinion of herself. She wrote, and I quote: 'I bow in accuracy and meticulousness and decency to no one. That is the reason I have survived as a star all these years – that and because in my field I am the best and the brightest there is.' She then called herself the queen of New York, as well as 'a class act loaded with prestige'.

Even in a town full of comedians, Suzy's opinion of her little old self had everyone rolling on the floor. The one who laughed the loudest, however, was Revson, who was immediately invited to appear on the Johnny Carson show and has become a celebrity of sorts.

What does all this mean? Easy. People are so desperate to get away from the Democratic presidential suitors that they will remain riveted in their seats waiting for the next round between two rather silly people, or rather, one silly lady. Which is a good thing. After all, I prefer listening to Suzy, even when she gives evidence against me, than to that ghastly buffoon Jesse Jackson. And as I write this I see Suzy has now compared herself to Mount Rushmore, and I do see a resemblance, except that she's somewhat older.

· A likely story (Highland life) ·

Elgin · Unlike Ralph Glasser's classic autobiography of growing up in the Gorbals, this is a not so classy confession about my Scottish school-days at Gordonstoun, a time that shall live in infamy, for it is those days I have been rebelling against ever since.

Yes, it's true, it was Gordonstoun that made me, not Olympus High, nor Eton, although that came about as a result. And it was my daddy who had the brilliant idea of sending me to Scotland 'to get educated'. In fact, I remember it as if it were yesterday. 'This boy is obviously worthless,' he told my mother one bright Athenian morning, 'so why not send him to that school near the North Pole where Prince Philip went. You never know, he too might make a good marriage'.

And so I was packed off to Scotland, to a borstal for the upper classes rather, something that crossed my mind years later when I attended graduate school at Pentonville. The first things that struck me were the surroundings and the weather. They were flat and wet, and it was extremely cold. The second was the food, which made me wonder, like Dr Johnson, why we were being fed food the rest of Europe only fed to horses. The third was a red-haired boy in the bunk next to me who kept drinking some foul-smelling stuff out of a bottle and who spent most of his time sleeping. His name was Anthony Haden-Guest.

The school was housed in a very old and solid Scottish Baronial building, one that belonged to the Gordon-Cumming family, I believe, until one of its members began punting on chemmy with the then Prince of Wales. We all wore short trousers and matching sweaters, blue in the morning and grey in the afternoon, with medal ribbons denoting what rank one had reached (unnecessary in Haden-Guest's case). The boy who bunked on my other side, however, resembled a Soviet marshal on Mayday. He had more ribbons than a Southern belle, as he was a great rugger player and rather useful (as they say in England) on the cricket pitch. His name was Humphrey Wakefield, now Sir Humphrey, a fact I wish I had known back then. I say this because rather than follow the example of Humphrey I

took after Haden-Guest, which Anthony himself admitted was like having Frank Giles as a role model.

Our daily routine would have been approved by Leonidas of Sparta as well as by Genghis Khan. When we were allowed to go to Elgin (the nearest town and one named after the man who very wisely preserved our marbles) there were no brothels to be found. Only pubs. For a hot-blooded Greek this was simply torture. The rest of the boys did not seem to mind in the least. Mind you, there was no hanky-panky either. Since the weather, the short pants and the chapped knees discouraged the homosexual intimacies universal in other public schools, there was little to worry about on that front. But it did make most of us feel left out of the rest of the British public school system, and I guess it still does.

One got beaten for honourable offences at Gordonstoun, offences such as hang-gliding over a mountain, or swimming under the ice, etc. ... Haden-Guest was the only boy in the school who was never beaten. Years later Spiro Niarchos matched his record by obtaining a doctor's certificate disqualifying him from all physical exercise. The doctor who issued it is at present living on his yacht off Monte Carlo. As is the kindly Scot who opened the first and last brothel in Elgin. Which reminds me. Ever since Gordonstoun I've made many Scottish friends, too numerous to mention here, in fact, and the only thing I regret is that it all ended in tears when I was expelled. It was on a Sunday, the brothel was shut, as all good brothels are on Sundays, and I happened to make a pass at a local girl who unfortunately turned out to be a Shetland pony. That is how I came to go to Eton.

· Fawn raider ·

Washington · Along with the forsythia, the pansies were out in force last week, as were the hacks of the White House press corps, for this was the 74th annual White House correspondents' dinner at the local inn that bears Mr Hilton's name.

Perhaps inn is the wrong word. The ballroom alone holds 3,000 people, and it was packed the night of the dinner with ink-stained wretches, electronic media persons and – for lack of a better word – politicians. Like last year, I was the guest of Arnaud de Borchgrave, editor of the *Washington Times*, the newspaper that did not give us Janet Cooke or that other great novelist, Bob Woodward.

Mind you, this is not to say that Arnaud is not the giving type. Far from it. He gave me my start in journalism 21 years ago and this time outdid himself by giving me the opportunity to escort a certified enchantress, a woman of such rare qualities and looks it would take sonneteers working three shifts plus overtime to describe her, a shredder of such dexterity she could dispose of the records of Kennedy and Biden quicker than one can say the word plagiarism. Needless to say, my date for the evening was Fawn Hall, and in a mini-skirt, to boot. To say that when given the news I jumped for joy would be an understatement on a par with that of Hitler's, who when asked in Hell what he would do if he had his life to live over again replied, 'Next time no more nice guy.'

Alas, things did not turn out as planned. First of all Miss Hall discovered that I was a journalist, and worse, a Greek journalist. She was then told that I am not confined by fact and that sometimes I make things up. Which meant that even if I looked like Errol Flynn and had the mind of Raymond Carr, my chances with her were those of a female hooker in San Francisco. My Waterloo came when I revealed to her that I have a dog called Oliver and that I named it after the good colonel. The look on her face said, 'You people will stoop to anything.' And matters got worse. In my desperation I asked her to marry me and was turned down faster than the French army retreated in 1940.

Well, you can't win them all; perhaps next year. In the meantime,

Ronald Reagan was in the finest of forms. For someone who has been accused by the liberals of being unable to ad-lib a cough without a cue card, he certainly did a hell of a job. The best joke of the night was not told by him, however. It's about Jesse Jackson's first act upon becoming president. He will proclaim his birthday a national holiday, as well as those of Michael Jackson and Reggie Jackson (a baseball player). Also 25 March. Why 25 March? Because it's the day the new Cadillacs come out.

Arnaud's tables were filled with political heavyweights, people such as Chief of Staff Howard Baker, Alexander Haig, John Warner and Jack Kemp, but most eyes were on my dinner companion. Afterwards I took Fawn to meet the sainted editor and the ex-sainted one, which in a way helped me save face a bit. Then it was off to bed because the next day I was invited to the White House for lunch. But before you get the wrong idea, the invitation did not come from the present occupants of 1600 Pennsylvania Avenue. My host was Peter Robinson, a speech-writer for President Reagan and a charming and very intelligent young man. When he rang to invite me I told him that I was hardly a favourite of Nancy Reagan in view of the fact that I poke fun at her lap-dog Jerry Zipkin every week. 'Never mind,' said Peter, 'we'll wait on the lawn until she and the President fly off to Camp David.' Which we did, and then the mother of my children and I were given a tour of the place and a delicious lunch.

It was my second time inside the great house, and this time I couldn't help causing a little mischief. I wrote a *risqué* note, put it in an envelope, and dropped it underneath my chair. I signed it Jerry Zipkin.

· At the barricades ·

I wish to say a few words about 7 May 1968, a day that saw the Parisian jet-set turn revolutionary, if only for a night. The night came to mind first because of Régine's autobiography (which I read in order to review) and second because as I lie awake longing for sleep I am watching Soviet TV on Channel 4 and a programme about the merry month of May 20 years ago.

It was a warm and pleasant Parisian night, and I was dining with a beautiful Brazilian girl whose only handicap was her politics. Needless to say we got into an argument about the 'student revolt' and for a while it looked as if she would do a Fawn Hall on me. Back then, however, I had more guts, so I decided to stay and argue the night away rather than tell her what I really thought of her and stick her with the bill. (Nothing diverts a girl's mind from dialectics of the Left like having to pay the bill.) The fact that she was awfully pretty also helped.

So, after dinner, I suggested we have a drink over at New Jimmy's, Régine's fabled boîte on the Boulevard Montparnasse. When the student uprising had begun the week before, I remember going out and buying an E-type Jaguar for its flashiness. Having seen what so-called Marxist-Leninists had done in my country and the rest of Eastern Europe, I felt so disgusted with the bourgeoisie acting like revolutionaries I decided my only course of action should be to provoke.

As luck would have it, no sooner had we reached the Boulevard Raspail than we were stopped at a road-block and confronted by students asking for money for their struggle. Now, I do not claim to be a brave man, but I knew that even one centime would cost me Gidgy, especially after the fiery speech I had given her during dinner while still in the safety of the Right Bank.

When asked, therefore, I gathered the little courage I had left, tried to look as sincere as possible, and announced that I would rather die for my principles than give them money for theirs. To my delight they waved me through, even using the formal *vous*. Gidgy looked like the cat that had swallowed the proverbial you-know-what.

Once inside New Jimmy's, we told the story to Régine, whose politics are similar to mine and who agreed that it was ironic to see Prague students demonstrating in order to achieve what those show-offs were denouncing outside her doors. Which led to yet another discussion about the courage of the demonstrators, and me telling her to allow me back in if things got out of hand outside. I then went out to see the revolution from up close. And saw that things did get out of hand, at least by Western standards.

So I walked back as calmly as possible, knocked on the famous black door with the Judas-hole and asked to be admitted. But as I was going in, a William Tell-like member of the CRS (the feared riot squad) fired two tear-gas grenades inside. You can imagine the rest. The place was already packed with humanity, and notorious for its lack of oxygen, which Régine always claimed made for a good night-club atmosphere. With two tear-gas bombs it turned into something not even Dante would dare try and describe.

Worse, when the jet-setters finally decided to exit Missolonghi-like, the CRS were waiting for them outside and began to club them at will (only a few upper-class Englishmen enjoyed it). Régine closed up her place following that evening, and now I read in her opus that she only opened her door because I was begging her to and she was afraid I might die of fright. Obviously one of the two of us is speaking with forked tongue.

· Splendour on the grass ·

I hadn't thought of it until I walked around SW19 on opening day last Monday. It's been 20 years since Wimbledon opened its doors to the pros, thus ensuring the only good thing to come out of the lousiest year of a disastrous decade. Just think.

French and American students were revolting against a system their Czech counterparts were willing to fight Soviet tanks bare-handed in order to achieve. Bobby Kennedy, the most ruthless member of an ambitious and ruthless family, was running for the US Presidency as an anti-war candidate, the very same war his brother and he had inflamed by ordering the assassination of South Vietnamese President Diem. The Tet Offensive had completely wiped out the Vietcong as a military force, yet the press had reported it in a manner that ensured the war would go on by presenting it as a victory.

Finally, the most intolerant and selfish generation in modern history, the hippy one, became associated in everyone's mind with love and peace and flower power. It was humbug time all around except where open tennis was concerned. In fact, it was one of the few idealistic principles to emerge from that ghastly period.

The first thing that strikes one watching today's players is their robotic approach to the game. No one, not even the Italians, seems to enjoy the game any longer. The women are even worse. Once upon a time it was the fair sex that led the 'it's a fun game' approach to tennis. Little Mo, Shirley Fry, Margaret Dupont, Darlene Hard and certainly the divine Maria Bueno and La Goolagong were living proof that life does extend beyond tennis.

No longer. The aggressiveness and single-mindedness that is required in order to be competitive is etched in their faces as sure as the sins of Dorian Gray were on his portrait. Ditto the men, although in their case it shows less. And it's the root of all envy that is the cause.

In the good (bad) old days of shamateurs, Wimbledon was the only tournament that did not pay under-the-table money. It paid expenses, rather. Thus a player who came all the way from Argentina and lost in the first round was paid more than one from Germany who got to the final. That did not stop Budge Patty and Jaroslav Drobny, both of whom are still proud possessors of the first penny they ever made, from battling on for five hours in order that one of them should advance to the quarter-finals. Nor did it deter Pancho Gonzales, a man who would long consider whether to give up his money or his life if someone demanded either, from winning 22–24, 1–6, 16–14, 6–3, 11–9 over Charlito Pasarell in 1969, before big money and the tie-break made tennis a television spectacle.

And speaking of television, it has probably done far more damage than Connors and McEnroe put together where sportsmanship is concerned. The reason is very simple. Disqualification in a case like McEnroe's is virtually impossible. Sponsors would not tolerate it, and without sponsors modern tennis is dead. And if tennis dies, a hell of a lot of businesses – billion-dollar businesses – would suffer. This no one in their right mind is about to allow to happen just because some American vulgarian is shouting obscenities at a helpless ump.

Yes, Wimbledon was instrumental in bringing us open tennis, and it did it for the right reasons, but I hope for its sake it won't one day regret it. If I know human nature and what the root of all envy does to it, the grass will one day have to go if the All England Club wishes to continue as a major championship. Grass suits very few of the major players, and the day will come when they will stay away, or choose to play an exhibition for more money in a far-away place. If this happens, and I still happen to be around, I will at least be able to blame it on 1968.

· Sob stories ·

Charles Benson was the first English man to befriend me upon my arrival on these shores, and despite a quarter of a century's hard drinking I remember the circumstances clearly. Even back then Benson had a seismographic alertness to people with money, and he relieved me of mine in no time at all. Something to do with his sick mother who was in desperate need of an operation that could only be performed in California. The next thing I knew the horse had come in last and his father was feeling poorly also.

Although Benson claimed to have been at Eton with me, I did not remember him, but I nevertheless continued to sponsor him for the next decade or so because of the people I was able to meet through him. Such gentlemen of the turf as Ted the Tulip, Fred (Three Fingers) Binns, and, last but not least, his flatmate, Philip Martyn, a.k.a. Filipo Martini or Felipe Martinez, as the situation warranted.

It was a wonderful time while it lasted, as they say, and it lasted until Benson decided to get married for the second time. (By then I had put both his sons from a previous marriage through Eton, and had managed to meet Madame Rosa of Shepherd Market, too.) A small problem arose with the seating at the grand luncheon he gave following the nuptials. His other major sponsor, the Aga Khan, was strangely reluctant to break bread with Taki, and this presented Benson with the first real dilemma of his life. Needless to say, he solved it in Solomonic fashion by placing his mother and me at a tiny table for two behind a curtain not too far away from the action. And with tears in his eyes he explained to me that under English custom the most honoured guest sat with the mother of the groom but not in view of the rest of *'les invitées'*. I remember having a bit of a blub upon hearing it.

This was ten years ago. Benson went legit. almost immediately after his marriage, and even began to go around with royals, an unheard-of breach of protocol for the rest of us. But because of his legendary charm all was forgiven, until last week, that is. This is when I visited my favourite bookshop and, lo and behold, saw Benson's incredibly pink and bloated countenance staring back at me from the shelves. His autobiography is titled *No Regard for Money*, which should ensure its immortality along with those two other classics of disinformation, *Why Jews Are my Favourite People*, by Adolf Hitler, and *Compassion is my Middle Name*, by Lavrenti Beria.

Not content with the omission of the words *Other People's* in the title, Benson then goes on to make me a lifelong enemy by referring to me only in passing (page 130) and accusing me of leaking an item to Nigel Dempster while on board the *QEII* on a transatlantic passage. This from a man – and I have it on the highest authority – who was instrumental in causing the power cuts of 1973 by his excessive use of the telephone while leaking items to various gossip columnists in exchange for the odd fiver.

Even worse, when I ran into him during a pro-am tennis tournament last week, he not only didn't apologize, he cheerfully asked me for a tenner and shoved a copy of his *opus* in my tennis bag.

Well, I am not surprised. With the kind of people my ex-friend Charles (Dickens) Benson sees nowadays, it would be almost impossible to keep up certain standards. Mind you, I am not alone in thinking this. Last Sunday, while dining *chez* Benson, I noticed his mantelpiece resembled a lunar surface, only barer. So I asked him whether he was going to the two rather smart balls I shall be attending this week, and he looked nonplussed. Being beastly to Taki in print has done for his social life what carrying an envelope through customs did for mine not so long ago. I shall be thinking of him while dancing this Wednesday, and the two Saturdays that follow.

· Don Gabriele ·

Siena · Gabriele D'Annunzio is my favourite Italian. A great poet and patriot, all he thought about was women. Although short and a cripple, with one eye, he nevertheless managed to seduce every beautiful woman of his time, but his Don Giovanni syndrome is not the reason he hasn't been given his due by those who'd rather think than fight. It's because he liked the trains to run on time.

The *mauvaises langues* have it that he fell in love with his pilot after he paper-bombed Fiume, but I don't buy it. In fact it would have been impossible as it's been mathematically proved that only pinkoes and commies turn queer after school. When my fellow Greek, Dallas Athena, revealed that Picasso was a bit of a poof, I wasn't surprised. Pablo, after all, was a man of the Left.

This week I had planned a pilgrimage to the Vittoriale, the poet's pleasure dome near Lake Garda, in order to introduce my seven-year-old to D'Annunzio, but the heat wave was used as an excuse by his mother to keep John-Taki in communist-run Tuscany. Leave it to a woman to try and shield a seven-year-old boy from D'Annunzio's influence.

I wonder what D'Annunzio would have thought of sexual liberation, singles bars, militant feminism, artificial insemination, and computer-dating services? Better yet, what would he have done with Miss Andrea Dworkin if he had read in her book *Intercourse* that 'Most men who make love to women make war on women because intercourse remains a means or the means of physiologically making a woman inferior.' I imagine he might have seduced her and made her change her mind, or – because he could be cruel at times – punish her by not laying a hand on her.

Needless to say, seduction has been too much on my mind lately. I guess it's the Tuscan atmosphere that must have something to do with it, or perhaps it is the hospitality of Lord Lambton, my friend and neighbour. For example: this week I went over for lunch and was seated between a beautiful mother and her 17-year-old daughter. To my surprise, as well as that of the mother of my children who was watching me like a hawk, I preferred the mother. It was her

voice that seduced me. The lady in question lives in Ireland, has three daughters and a very nice husband who she's happily married to. My task is a hard one, but I really only want to hear her voice. By the end of lunch she had agreed to accept my telephone calls and read out the Irish telephone book if need be.

Incidentally, during that very lunch I sat across from a lovely lady by the name of Isabel Colegate. She is married to a friend of mine, Michael Briggs, and like all talented people she never once mentioned the fact that she, too, does a bit of scribbling. Which meant that all through the lunch I spoke about nothing but yours truly, and felt a bit of a jerk once I realized who the lady was.

Oh, well, nobody's perfect, and it got worse that night. Jasper and Camilla Guinness were driving over for dinner, so once again my host requested my company after Jasper had expressed a desire for some light entertainment. Serendipitously, two lovely girls happened to drop by. One of them was a tall blonde English girl I had met once before but much too briefly, the other an American from Los Angeles, of all places. My hostess, Claire Ward, kindly put me between them and, even if I say so myself, I didn't do too badly. My plan was a simple one. By playing the clown I thought I had a chance with Los Angeles, Jeffrey Bernard having once told me a blonde secretary from that hellhole had taken him to her bed when he passed out on her shoulder.

Unfortunately, what worked for Jeff did not for Taki. When I made my move she (LA) declared that if I wasn't such a clown I might have had a chance with her, but not tonight, thank you. In a panic I turned to the English girl but that Brutus also let me down. It had something to do with being asked second, I imagine.

· A wreath too soon ·

St Moritz · It is so beautiful up here this time of year I expect Julie Andrews to pop up any moment and sing out that the hills are alive with the sound of music. It is green, cool, uncrowded and healthy. And it's free.

The last time I was in this resort I was also staying with my present host, Gianni Agnelli, and was literally run out of town. It was 1964 and the King of Greece, King Paul, was on his last legs. Gianni was in Turin working and he would ring at night and get the day's gossip. St Moritz was very lively that year as it was the only place in Europe that had had a snowfall. While gossiping away over the telephone Gianni told me that the King had had it. He meant it metaphorically and I took it literally. After hanging up I rang various Greeks and announced that the King was dead. They in turn got on to their various flunkeys in the Olive Republic and within minutes hundreds of wreaths began to arrive in the palace of Tatoi. There was only one minor trouble. King Paul was still very much alive, and he and his strong-willed wife, Queen Frederika, did not see the joke. The rich Greeks who had attached their names to the expensive wreaths were told in no uncertain terms what the royal couple thought of their haste.

You can imagine the rest. Tina Onassis played Sam Spade and traced the 'joke' back to me. Billionaires, and Greek billionaires in particular, do not like being made fools of. They were really out for blood, and not even Avvocato Agnelli's declaration that it had been a misunderstanding made any difference. So I did the only thing one has to do in such circumstances. I remained closeted in my room and announced that I had meant it as a joke from the start, and I would do it all over again. Then, after a decent interval, I flew back to Gstaad and walked up the various mountains.

But for any of you who may have been incarcerated in Albania for the last 50 years, a brief background of Gianni Agnelli is in order. Although the Italian monarchy was abolished in 1946, the crown, in reality, was simply transferred from the house of Savoy to that of Agnelli. It is not only the richest house, 30 billion smackers the last time I counted, it is the house that sets the standards in a country that worships style. And no one has more style, looks or charm than Gianni Agnelli. I first met him on the Riviera 30 years ago, and although he has always worked hard, back then he also played hard. I quickly became his Leporello.

Then we both got serious. He became Europe's *numero uno* tycoon, and I turned into an intellectual. We rarely saw each other as he was busy running Italy and I was hard at work on my thesis on leisure. This week, however, it was nostalgia time. Early Monday morning I drove to Florence and boarded a train for Milan. Once there I was whisked up the Engadine by an Agnelli driver and into his private Falcon jet. In two hours we had landed in Santiago de Compostela, in north-western Spain. We did a quick tour of the magnificent cathedral and then drove to the coast where we boarded probably the most beautiful sailing boat in the world, definitely the fastest as far as cruising sailboats are concerned. It is a 120-foot sloop, a J-class aluminium beauty with a 150-foot mast that Gianni had built at Abeking Rasmussen this year. She has a teak deck, a light white wooden interior and a crew of ten. In very light winds we sailed at ten knots. In moderate conditions we reached 14 easily, and the boat is capable of doing 20 or perhaps even more.

The next morning we sailed down to Vigo, a wonderfully ramshackle city that reminded me of Europe before the developers, where we sailed until late afternoon, when once again we boarded Gianni's aeroplane and in an hour and a half – due to strong winds – we had landed in St Moritz. It may sound in bad taste, but it is the only way to travel. Last week I made a valiant effort to fly to London in order to meet loyal *Spectator* readers, and not only did I get stuck in Pisa airport for more than three hours, I also crashed my brand new car trying to be on time. What I should have done is call Gianni. Now, there's a man the airlines have never pushed around.

· Hair-raiser ·

Siena · Even if I say so myself, my birthday party was a great success. The trick was having the orchestra play nothing which separates the sexes. There were foxtrots, rumbas, cha-cha-chas and lots of tangos, but no Zulu music. Zulu music was intended to inspire savages to fight, not to love, yet people insist on playing it in discos, nightclubs, and the occasional stately home. Zulu music is responsible for most of the world's ills, including drugs and football violence. It has lowered the standards of civilized behaviour, and has given us Yoko Ono, Keith Richards, this Springsteen horror and – worst of all – the flower-power peace bums of the Sixties. I know for a fact that the ghastly Ceausescu listens to it, as does Ortega and the bearded Cuban butcher. They say that Major Ron is a closet listener, especially when in London. Our beloved Prime Minister, however, has never even heard of Elvis Presley.

But I digress. The only sour note of my birthday bash was when a young whippersnapper defended the right of Lew Wasserman (the greedy and ghastly head of MCA) to finance a film that depicts our Lord Jesus more of this world than the next. As the party was in my house, and a guest is almost sacred in a Greek home, I chose to ignore the provocation. The next day I read Paul Johnson's brilliant piece saying that we should show people that blasphemy doesn't pay by staying away from Wasserman products, and felt a lot better. Until I read that in Noo Yawk and El Lay it was playing to standing room only. As Mandy once said, it would, wouldn't it?

My dinner was for 32, it was outdoors and with the orchestra playing. The gossip was all about a man cutting off his finger in a jealous rage over Katya Grenfell, as well as the bathing habits of our noble Lord Weidenfeld. It seems that Roger Middleton, a good friend of my friend Katya Grenfell, got so annoyed when an ageing Lothario kissed Katya while greeting her the night before that he went to his room and chopped off his middle finger. He was rushed to hospital where doctors managed to reattach it, although some *mauvaises langues* say that the finger was someone else's. The case of our noble lord is far clearer, if almost as gruesome.

He was staying at a house taken by two rich and ageing but very elegant American ladies, Mrs Bruce and Mrs Tree. No sooner had he arrived than a native reported he had seen an escaped baboon, and the fuzz arrived. Upon closer inspection of the property, the 'baboon' turned out to be nothing more lethal than our George, sunning himself in the nude. Apparently this noble lord's secret charm – published here for the first time – is that he is covered with hair from head to foot, including his buttocks. (This is a world exclusive.)

The last piece of gossip I have to report concerns yours truly. And it came via Desmond Guinness, who had just lunched with the two American ladies and our boy George. Weidenfeld was quoted as saying that Taki would never be able to get away with what I do if it weren't for the protection I get from four people: Gianni Agnelli, David Beaufort, Tony Lambton and John Aspinall. My answer is, what protection? I have gone to prison, been sued and taken to court, have had to pay through the nose, and dropped my last devalued drachmas in order for Aspers to feed his baboons. Sorry, gorillas as well. If these four friends of mine are providing protection, all four should change their name to Maginot.

But I do understand why the great publisher feels the way he does. After all, protection to him comes naturally. He married one of America's richest, La Payson, and now is friendly with an even richer one, La Getty. And my spies tell me he is interested in La Weymouth. Protection is his middle name, not mine.

· Not a bore we know ·

Oh boy, what a weekend I've just had up in Leicestershire with Princess Di and Fergie!! Although I am known to be the epitome of discretion, I'm afraid there will be some questions asked in the House whenever the sybarites who run our lives decide to get back to work.

And it's even more embarrassing because I now hear that this year it will be my rival who will be replacing his mother and opening Parliament. Oy veh, what is a poor Greek boy to do but get out of town come October. Mind you, I regret nothing because – as the great Barnaby Conrad once wrote – it was fun while it lasted.

But enough of holding back. Unlike Major Ron I will come clean, and to hell with the consequences. I went up to one of the most beautiful of counties for the wedding of Alex Dolbey to the delicious Susie Murray-Philipson, as did the Princess of Wales and the Duchess of York. Unfortunately, there were another 247-odd people doing the same thing, and although I didn't get to talk to or even see the two aforementioned ladies, I thought I'd drop their names as everyone else seems to be doing nowadays.

Perhaps our lack of contact was due to my having reverted to type and gotten blind drunk during the dinner that preceded the dance. By the time the Zulu music started to rock I was in no state to make the banal conversation one is supposed to make with royals, so I gave them both a miss. Others were not so fortunate, namely Cornelia, the sister of the bride. Cornelia Faulkner is as nice a girl as one can hope to find during the Eighties, yet even she did a Brutus on me and rolled her eyes upwards when a bore came up and asked her to dance while yours truly was in the middle of a long soliloquy. What she meant was, what took the bore so long?

Then there was Birdie Fortescue, just as nice as Cornelia, but just as treacherous towards me that night. And many others whose names escape me. Needless to say, it wasn't all my fault. Having passed the last month in the Olive Republic, I wasn't used to the wonderful but strong claret served by my host and it went down a bit too fast. The result was that I crashed my rented car into that of a friend and then, in the company of the soybean king of Chicago, went looking for

Bruern – my ex-ancestral country seat in Oxfordshire – thinking it was adjacent to the marquee.

This is not to say that the weekend was one long disaster for me. The opposite, in fact. Although I remember little of the dance, I did notice that during the reception Mr Tom King, the minister with the cushiest job in the Cabinet, raised his glass to his niece, the bride, and to her husband, and found it to be empty, as the best man, nervously waiting to give the next speech, had downed it along with his own.

Towards the end of the evening I managed to sober up and that is when I met a man I've wanted to meet for a long time. He is the brother of the bride, and his name is Hylton. The reason I've wanted to meet him is because of the remark he once made to Frau Kluge, who is now married to one of America's richest men. Mrs Kluge is a nice woman, but she suffers from an extreme case of royalitis. In fact, when she sees a royal – even Ronnie Ferguson – she tends to tremble, go weak at the knees, and all the rest of the things that afflict people who suffer from the disease. One day, in Virginia, where the Kluges keep a large house for expatriate Englishmen who have shaken hands with a royal, she announced that the King of Greece had just rung her from Europe and told her he and his party had shot 11 boars. 'Oh dear,' expostulated Hylton, 'I hope no one we know.'

Of course, there were no Kluges around that night, and I guess this is why Prince Philip didn't make it. But not to worry. It was a hell of a party despite some people's protestations to Harry Worcester to keep his boring friends (Christopher Gilmour and Taki) to himself. But something tells me it was my last wedding party for quite a while.

· We are not amused ·

One of the reasons I'm almost happy to be flying off to the Big Bagel is that I shall thus be missing the newspaper coverage of Fergie's return. Although I realize that news about the royals makes many suburbanites happy, the Fergie saga is getting too ridiculous for words. In fact, I'm getting pretty tired of the whole tribe. Royals should be like well-behaved children: seen occasionally but almost never heard, and they certainly should not be allowed to go on the idiot box.

Not that I disagree with what Prince Charles said – on the contrary – just with his right to say it. Royals appearing on the box will do for the institution of monarchy what General Curtis LeMay did for Tokyo's architecture in the early Forties. Just imagine if Fergie's hubby decided to emulate his older brother and asked for equal time in order to give us his views on the incredible lightness of you-know-Koo. Think how embarrassing it would be if that little squirt Linley was given an hour to harangue us about the incredible lightness of modern chairs (or his own, for that matter). Finally, and God forbid, what would happen if Ronnie Ferguson went on the air to complain about the collapsing standards of clubs and the incredible lightness of massages nowadays?

What would happen is that England would become the laughing stock of the Western world, a position now firmly held by the Olive Republic, thanks to Papandreou and his bimbo. Incidentally, when Lord Carrington asked Papandreou last summer whether he was pleased the Democrats had nominated Dukakis, Papadoc turned purple: 'He's not really Greek,' he spluttered, 'and furthermore he's a friend of my wife.'

Mind you, being a republican, I'm hardly worried about the royal over-exposure, but at last I'm beginning to understand why Prince Charles insists on keeping the ban on Argie polo players. If Princess Di followed the example of Fergie's mother and sister, things could turn nasty. (A ten-year siege of Buenos Aires to get her back, followed by another ten-year peregrination around the Kalahari ... But I digress.)

When I was young I was a royalist. King George II led the fight against the dirty commies, as did his brother, King Paul, who succeeded him. What I didn't like was the fact that the Greek royals jumped when the Brits told them to. They left Greece because Churchill said so, leaving us behind to eat our dates and an occasional cat or dog. When Paul's son, Constantine, became King, aged four, it was only a matter of time before the Byzantine Greek political scene got the better of him. Constantine had some very good friends, but also some real lulûs. One of them, a smoothie by the name of Constantine Petalas, made Louis Basualdo seem decent by comparison. Half of Greek society was suffering from lumbago by the time Constantine lost his throne, due to excessive bowing and scraping. That is when I decided royalty was for the birds, and not for people with dignity.

Needless to say, I thoroughly approve of royals such as the Belgians, the Scandinavians, and even the Dutch. I particularly like the fact that last month the Swedes rejected King Carl Gustaf XVI's request for special parking privileges which would have speeded the picking up of his dry-cleaning and groceries. Well done, Sweden, for once. When Prince Philip and Princess Margaret get on their high horse, they should be sent by our sainted Prime Minister to Stockholm for a spell. It will teach them humility and better manners.

Last but not least, a word about the King of Spain. He has done a good job and he's a joy to behold, although his wife doesn't particularly like me. I sat next to her once on a Niarchos boat, and when I volunteered my political opinions she called me a pest three times. Once in Greek, once in English, and I assume the last thing she called me was pest in Spanish. At least I hope so.

· Beach boys ·

Delray Beach · Unlike in Palm Beach, its chic neighbour ten miles to the north, some things in Delray never change. For 76 years residents have strolled along Atlantic Avenue, the town's main street, greeting friends and strangers alike, as people used to do back in the good old days when manners were more important than money. For 76 years Delray has considered itself a neighbourhood community with a home-town atmosphere, an attitude that would bring on instant social leprosy to anyone affecting it, ten miles north of here.

The very first time I drove through the place was in 1954, and I was the proud owner of a black Thunderbird convertible, the latest Ford model of that year. I stopped for a reason. It was a Sunday, I was on my way to Miami Beach and it was the first time I had seen people actually walking in a Florida street rather than driving. I remember it very clearly. There were family outings on the beach, the churches were full and after the services there were volleyball games at the beach and children made human chains in the waves. Thirty-four years later, very little has changed.

I have been going down to Delray for the last four Thanksgiving weekends and staying at a wonderfully old-fashioned beach-club motel called the Seagate. The owner is a gent, which makes for the friendliness of the place, and he has two truly beautiful daughters, which needs no explanation. Alas, his elder one, Amanda, a gifted writer, got married last Saturday, making it a sad occasion for the countless suitors who have been sniffing round the place for the last five years. Amanda gave a terrific party and flew down the man people are calling the Cole Porter of the Eighties, Christopher Mason, a Brit with talent galore.

Mason doesn't bite the hand that feeds him, but he certainly teases it, in verse and on the piano. Here's an example of his wit, on the prosperati's most egregious couple:

Now the Gutfreunds are good friends of mine,
John and Susan are simply divine.

> *As people they're good, they're just misunderstood*
> *And their pure sense of style is sublime.*
> *And if Salomon Brothers is waning, and Susan is getting too grand,*
> *The Gutfreunds are darling young people.*
> *Oh, why can't New York understand?*

I rediscovered Delray because my friend Chuck Pfeiffer's parents live down here. Chuck and I run each morning on the beach, swim for as long as we run and then play tennis. In between sports Chuck regales the tourists with stories about the people he's killed (two silver stars in Nam). It makes for an empty beach and lots of room in the patio where we lunch. This year my best friend in Chicago flew down – the pork-belly king of that town, incidentally – Christopher Gilmour. The pork-belly king protested at Pfeiffer's stories as they kept the women away, but we still managed to have a whale of a time. On Friday evening we got so wrecked we drove to Palm Beach and went into Cartier's thinking it was a bookstore. Incidentally, there are 150 jewellery shops in Palm Beach for each book boutique.

That's the bad news. The good is that there is only one Bath and Tennis club. It's the best club of its kind in the world, and the tennis atmosphere about as good as you can find. The club is not only exclusive, it's also restricted, which means minorities need not apply. As I was playing rather well I drew a crowd. Afterwards, however, I found out it was because some new members thought I was black and Jewish, to boot.

· Yule *nouvelle* ·

New York · This is a particularly gay time to be in New York (I use the word gay in its correct and original meaning) with parties galore and Christmas trees and decorations sprouting up all over the city. The birth of our Lord Jesus is big business over here, and Bagel-dwellers pull out all the stops come December. Even the muggers get into the spirit of things. Last week an old lady was robbed by a man who held a knife covered with red and green ribbons to her throat.

Christmas aside, the arrival of Michael and Raisa has everyone up in arms, no pun intended. Store owners have been complaining for weeks that the security arrangements will be bad for business, while law-abiding citizens (a minority in this town) have been worried that the bad guys will have a field day while the cops guard Gorby and the missus. As it turned out, Gorby's visit was good for business, and good for the bad guys too.

Needless to say, 'nouvelle society' – as *Women's Wear* has dubbed the latest *nouveaux riches* and the extremely greedy – has not exactly been hibernating. The charity party scam is on full throttle, and hardly a day goes by without the gossip columns gushing over such elegant ladies as Mrs Saul Steinberg, Mrs Henry Kravis, Mrs Donald Trump, Mrs Ann Bass, Mrs Sid Bass, Mrs Ann Trout and others too fishy to mention in the elegant pages of *The Spectator*.

And speaking of Henry Kravis, last week at Mortimer's I spotted him sitting on four cushions and lunching with some other Liliputians (rumour has it that no one taller than five foot five is allowed to approach him) and I tried to stick my lunch bill on his tab, but was restrained from doing so by an outraged owner.

Two weeks ago, during a dinner given by Rupert Murdoch, Zipkin struck again. To the astonishment of everyone he appeared to be challenging Arnaud de Borchgrave over a point of etiquette which is like me trying to give Malcolm Muggeridge a lesson in celibacy. Borchgrave is a count of the Holy Roman Empire, the editor of the *Washington Times*, one of the greatest foreign correspondents ever, and has impeccable manners, to boot. Like the gentleman that he is he said nothing, but was heard muttering, 'Isn't it astonishing that the face that lunched a thousand shits should presume to give us a lesson in manners?'

I guess it is not astonishing, not with *nouvelle* society around. This weekend Sid Bass is marrying Mercedes Tavacoli, a Persian lady. Bass just paid about 200 million smackers to divorce his wife in order to marry the Persian Mercedes, and will spend almost as much for the ball he is giving at the Met on Saturday. For some strange reason Sid and Mercedes did not invite Taki, but invited Mrs Taki, which must be a first even for *nouvelle* society. Mrs Taki did not want to go, but I insisted. Thankfully there is another wedding party that night, one that I'm taking my two 20-year-old girlfriends to.

1989

· Sobering up ·

New York · I don't know about you, but I badly need a rest from the holidays. The nights between Christmas and the New Year are known to be dangerous to one's health, especially in the Big Bagel, where whooping it up is almost as big a business as the charity scam. My physical collapse began with my house party on Christmas Eve. For reasons I cannot divulge, I drank too much fire-water much too early in the day, and by the time dinner was over I was able to do a better imitation of Anthony Haden-Guest than the 'beast' himself. The wife didn't help matters. She insisted on playing Sherlock Holmes throughout the evening, checking up on the identity of various girls I had invited, and asking them questions not even El Al asks travelling Palestinians.

Mind you, it is very pleasant to get plastered in one's own house. Every time I do – which is often – I think of poor Jeff passing out in foreign places such as the Groucho Club or the Coach and Horses and cringe. By contrast, when he and I went drinking together and ended up back in my London flat, he passed out at five in the afternoon, woke up at five in the morning and joined the party that was going on full blast without realizing he had had a 12-hour rest in between vodka-and-limes.

Yes, such are the joys of drinking at home. Another who knows this all too well is Geoffrey Wheatcroft. Although he is known to pass out in far grander abodes than mine, he and I once went to sleep while discussing the meaning of life. (Or perhaps the meaning of a certain girl.) When my housekeeper discovered us in the morning she thought we were awake but deep in contemplation. We were only sitting very upright on the sofa, and only when our heads slowly began to touch did she realize we were both out cold.

No sooner had I recovered than it was time to get into shape for pre-New Year's Eve celebrations. Unfortunately, I am not as strong as I once used to be, and they left me feeling rather flat on the night that counted. Nevertheless I gave a good account of myself at the wonderful party Reinaldo and Carolina Herrera gave, although I must admit some of the guests who didn't know me thought I was speaking Swahili toward the end.

And speaking of guests, I met Ken Tynan's widow, Kathleen Tynan, that night, and she turned out to be great fun despite the fact she's such a dirty commie pinko. Tynan is a friend of Fidel Castro, I believe, so I had to remind her that it was 30 years ago that the bearded butcher took over Havana. I remember it well, as my friend Zographos burst into my room at the Gstaad Palace and announced that our Havana nights were over. It was terrible news, as bad as when Zographos had announced that Marshal Papagos had outlawed all the brothels in Greece back in 1953. But do you think there were any demonstrations outside the Cuban legation to mark the 30th anniversary of Castro's rule in that dismal prison-land? Of course not. On the contrary, the romantic infatuation of many intellectuals and Hollywood trained seals continues unabated. (Some did, however, write him a letter.)

Oh, well, it is now 1989, and I have made some resolutions. One of them is never to write about politics in a 'High life' column again, and certainly never again to refer to anyone I don't agree with politically as a *malakas* (Greek for wanker). I have also sworn never to drink again, chase young girls, gamble, smoke and waste time. No more Annabel's, no more Tramps, no more Nell's, no more Mortimer's, and no more anti-Sandinista rhetoric. Nineteen eighty-nine will be a year of healing, as they say, and if you believe this you're bound to believe that Castro will resign because some pointy-heads asked him to.

· Who'd fancy Nancy? ·

New York · Mike Wallace is an acne-ravaged 71-year-old mediacrat with dyed black hair who is an expert at kicking people who are on their way down. Wallace works for CBS, the television network that did more to undermine the war in Vietnam than China and the Soviet Union combined. Seven years ago Wallace hoodwinked General Westmoreland into doing an interview and then, by expert cutting of the film, accused him of deliberately misleading his government by cooking the intelligence books on Vietcong strength.

Westmoreland, needless to say, had done nothing of the kind, but libel laws being what they are in America, the good general could not prove that Wallace had done it with malice aforethought.

Wallace also did a hatchet job on the fallen Shah, while treating him with less politeness than he presumably would have extended to Joe Stalin. On the other hand, when Mike interviewed Khomeini, he bowed and scraped in a manner that would have embarrassed Uriah Heep. Last Sunday he surpassed his Khomeini performance while interviewing Fancy Nancy Reagan, a lady who, I presume, disapproves of the manner the Virgin Mary dressed in her time, despite the fact that designer dresses were then a thing of the future.

Now, I have often written badly of La Nancy, a lady I have never met, but had any of you seen the Wallace interview I am sure you would agree with me that the women's vote should be revoked in America, and the sooner the better. Wallace, who is an old friend of the fancy one, was as gentle in his questions as, say, I would be had I to interview Oliver North, a man whom La Nancy made clear she does not like. Now, the idea that a woman whose two best friends are one Jerry Zipkin and Alecko Papamarkou, a Greek who took three years of elocution lessons in order to learn to speak like Tallulah Bankhead, can judge two war heroes like North and Poindexter seems to me as outrageous as having Pol Pot run an orphanage.

Nancy, my spies tell me, was the first to ask her hubby to throw the two patriots to the wolves, and for that act alone I hope she never again gets to wear Bill Blass. Alas, It was not the only time she meddled. As that arch-phoney Mike Deaver conceded in his memoirs, Nancy was working full-time behind the scenes to end aid to the anti-communist forces in Nicaragua. Even worse, she was in league with the likes of Armand Hammer, the only man I know who has managed to con both Joe Stalin and Prince Charles.

Nancy's best remarks were about how she hoped that she would be remembered. Not for her fondness for fancy clothes and Hollywood moguls, nor for her use of astrologers, but for her efforts to solve the nation's social problems. I must say I had a hell of a laugh at that one, a laugh that was heard all the way down to Mortimer's, a place Nancy pledged she will visit soon and as often as possible.

Well, the country does need laughs, and Wallace provided it with our now ex-First Lady. Which proved to me yet again that a stretch limo, an anti-Contra attitude and a public relations huckster as mentor will keep chic liberal hacks like Wallace off one's back – in fact on their knees. This week I'm off to the nation's capital to dance away the nights celebrating the coming of Barbara Bush to Washington as *numero uno*. And next week I will report to you what it was like to be near the President of the United States without a Zipkin in sight.

· Suite success ·

Washington · As everyone who has ever been to Beverly Hills knows, the shorter and balder the producer, the taller and more buxom the blonde. Come inauguration time this principle also applies to hotel suites. At the Ritz Carlton, the poshest of the posh watering holes of the nation's capital, the best suite went for 15,000 big ones, and the smallest billionaire in the world, Monsieur Henry Kravis, was the lucky man to get his bid in first.

Needless to say it was the penthouse suite he got, and the *mauvaises langues* immediately began to speculate whether the management had substituted the furniture for miniatures in order to make him feel more at home. I was ensconced on the fourth floor, in a nice double room that cost somewhat less than the Soviet Union's annual military budget, the reason for this being that there were no celebrities staying on my floor. Well, none if you don't include the queen of cream, Mrs Estée Lauder, there with her son Ronald, currently running for mayor of the Big Bagel.

Another great man staying at the Ritz was Donald Trump, or 'The Donald', as his Czechoslovak wife calls him. There were rumours that The Donald would try and buy the Ritz and everyone staying in it, but to the best of my knowledge they were just that. Not even Trump can buy Kravis and Lauder and half the state of Texas, which at times seemed to be staying at the hotel. What turned out not to be a rumour was the wonderful service the Ritz continued to provide although bursting at the seams.

My host, Arnaud de Borchgrave, editor-in-chief of the *Washington Times*, the best paper in town and not to be confused with the mendacious *Washington Post* of Janet Cooke fame, proved something of a miracle man by getting me and two teenagers of the fair sex invited to the most exclusive of parties. In fact, so exclusive was the last one I attended that the mendacious *Post* described it in a headline as, 'Last Dance at the Ritz'. It then gushed that 'it was the party to end all parties. Literally'. The bash was given by Mary Jane Wick, Fancy Nancy's best friend, and Buffy Cafritz, a socialite in the District of Columbia. It included every heavy hitter and, again

RITZ
CARLTON

WATER →

in the words of the mendacious *Post*, 'the famous and the even more famous'. As far as I could tell it was a hell of a party, first of all because it included the Bush family, but also because I heard the best remark of the week during dinner. I was sitting next to Jane Ikard, a lady journalist and big insider, and heard her say, 'Thank God the Bushes came in, and I don't have to have a new neck.' Mrs Ikard is of a certain age, and was referring to her wrinkles.

And speaking of wrinkles, I noticed that Barbara Walters had none, although she did have trouble eating her soup with her mouth closed. I also noticed Senator John Warner in a Taki state, and I made friends with Senators Wilson, Stevens and Laxalt. But my NBF (new best friend) is William Webster, head of the CIA, a man who spent the entire evening whispering to Arnaud de Borchgrave and his wife.

Given the fact that I was the only unknown in the room, I did get a bit tipsy, so much so in fact that when I spotted our noblest lord, George Weidenfeld, coming in with Lally Weymouth and five Israeli professors from Mossad University, I got up on a table and cheered loudly. That is when Arnold Scaasi, the Barbara Bush designer who was born Isaacs and now spells his name backwards, finally acknowledged me. He told me to sit down and to shut up.

· Elegy for my father ·

Athens · The only person I lied to when I got busted back in 1984 was my father. He first heard of it through the Greek newspapers and rang me at once. But I told him the stuff had been planted on me. I was too ashamed to tell him otherwise. Not afraid, mind you, but ashamed. He believed me without reservation. Ironically, some-one had planted dope on him during the German occupation and then given him away to the Gestapo, but that had been an obvious plant and he had been released almost immediately.

My father had a terrific Resistance record. He first fought in Albania with courage as an officer in the machine-gun corps and then financed and published the chief Resistance underground newspaper throughout the Nazi occupation. He had closed down his textile factories despite German threats, and he was the man who smuggled George Papandreou out of Athens and on to a wait-ing British submarine so he could head a Greek government-in-exile.

When the constant Anglo-American bombing would terrify me to tears, I still recall him looking disapprovingly at a six-year-old's fear. I vividly remember his coolness under fire, especially during the civil war. When the Reds blew up his factories, he never once complained. It was the bleak winter of 1944 and Athens was one great cemetery. Still, he foraged around and managed to get watches for my brother and me.

After I was thrown out of school in America for being violent, I spent a harrowing three days waiting for him to come and get me. I had seen his temper before and was not looking forward to it. But when he heard the reason for my dismissal, he smiled at me and said, 'I thought you had done something unmanly.' Throughout the next thirty years he complained constantly about my way of life, but continued to support me in style.

Last Friday morning, at 9.30, my mother rang to tell me my father had dropped dead getting out of bed. The news didn't regis-ter right away because I was still drunk from the night before. When it did, I broke down for probably the first time in more than forty years. I was not ashamed to do so, although he would have hated it.

My father had received the two highest decorations the Greek nation has to offer, one for bravery, the other for achievement. He never wore them, just as he never used a broken-down Venetian title his family was given long ago. He left home at fourteen because of a dispute with my grandfather. He was self-made and a gentleman of the old school. He took care of my wife as if she was his daughter, and he was a businessman who created jobs, not junk bonds. He had 5,000 workers in the Sudan, hundreds of sailors on his ships and hundreds employed in his hotels.

Ironically, it took me five years to write my prison book because I didn't want to hurt him with the truth. Just as I decided finally to come clean, he passed away. I had been extremely close to him the last ten years, in fact always, and can't remember a day that went by without me thinking of him and being proud. Two days before his death I watched *Voyage Round my Father*, and John Mortimer's words still ring in my ears: about how lonely one feels without a father, and in my case, how unprotected for the first time in my life.

On Monday morning, the Athens heat wave subsided and a cooling breeze helped my aged mother through the funeral ordeal. Once again, I was proud to be his son. The high and mighty all came, including the head of the government and most of parliament. But so did all the men and women who had once worked for him, including those of the fairer sex who frequent the night. There were many speeches. Then he was lowered into the family crypt, next to his German and Italian ancestors, and was gone for ever.

· Sir Harold's hospitality ·

Athens · My Tuscan friend and neighbour Lord Lambton (or Lorlambton, as my children call him) had a treat in store for me last week. 'But you'll have to be on time and wear a tie and jacket,' I was forewarned. So, while others more inclined toward glitz, megabucks and La Taylor sweated it out in Tangier paying homage to Malcolm Forbes, I drove the mother of my children and Tony Lambton to Florence to lunch with the grand old man of English letters, Sir Harold Acton.

Now it's not every day that a nightclub character like myself lunches with the likes of Sir Harold, but stranger things happen all the time: for example, decent and intelligent people like Bill Buckley and Gianni Agnelli having to sit down *chez* Forbes and break bread with, say, Leonard Stern and Henry Kravis, not to mention that God-awful publicity hound Lee Iacocca. (I had planned to refuse Malcolm's invitation, which incidentally got lost in the mail, on the grounds that I refuse to dine with La Graham of the mendacious *Washington Post*, Barbara Walters, Mort (the dork) Zuckerman and others too low-life to mention in these elegant pages.)

But back to high life, or better yet, higher thoughts. Upon meeting the great man for the first time I was reminded at once how standards have slumped. His manners are so natural, so impeccable and so wonderfully old-fashioned, that I never want to play against the Coach and Horses ever again, even at the Oval. But what was most impressive was his art of conversation. I had heard that he modelled his speech after that of the great Oscar, but now I ain't so sure. It was too perfect to be anything but a genuine individual style. And he certainly didn't mumble or try to be too lah-di-dah, because I suppose being natural is an old-fashioned way of showing good manners, an unheard-of thing nowadays.

And speaking of people being unnatural, I loved Sir Harold's way of escalating criticism about some rich American women who affect ladylike manners but who would hardly have been deemed ladies in a gentler age. He began by defending them when I called them a couple of social-climbing old bags, nodded his head in agreement when I said they were *sans noblesse*, and finally volunteered what terrific bores they were, 'bores with such superficial knowledge'.

Needless to say, it wasn't all gossip, but Sir Harold wished to make me feel at home so he kept the gravitas down to a minimum. Almost as good as his conversation were his food and his servants, and of course the wine.

After lunch we sat like Edwardians in a corner of the great room next to the library and had coffee. That is when Sir Harold, or my NBF, revealed to us that he's a lifelong reader of the *Spectator*, and I revealed to him that I have read his two-volume history of the Bourbons of Naples not once, not twice, but three times, and plan to read it once more.

It just so happened that it was the hottest day of the summer, yet the thick walls of the fifteenth-century villa La Pietra kept us cool throughout. The fantastic gardens were another matter. Both house and garden are too well known among aesthetes for me to describe, but I shall try and give a personal impression. Sir Harold's gardens do not allow natural features to stand free. Like Florence in the past, there is no room for robust independence. Anarchy plays no part in his world. It is the way things should be. Thank God my invitation to Tangier got lost.

· Chickening out ·

Athens · Just about now the weather is changing, and by the time I've had a long swim, shower, drink and lunch on board, it begins to get dark, windy and a bit chilly. My schedule is as precise as that of any commuter. Leave Piraeus for a late lunch on board on Friday, return late Sunday night, except when I go to Mykonos and manage to get lucky.

Greek sailors, among the best of a good breed, are notoriously conservative. They fear the elements more than their ancestors once upon a time feared the Gods. And this is why my captain loathes going to Mykonos. There are always strong winds blowing, which in the summer keep the place cool and the water clean. In the autumn things are different. Last weekend we had a rough crossing on 8 Beaufort and, as the boat can do 35 knots, for a while it felt as if we were in the middle of Hurricane Hugo. Then the captain wisely cut the speed to 26, and the girls on board gave thanks to Poseidon for the rest of the way.

Once in Mykonos Chuck Pfeiffer and I went out for a reconnaissance, and quickly realized we had just crossed the Aegean in order to attend a gay and lesbian convention. So we pulled up anchor and headed for Spetsai, an island I've really come to dislike.

Spetsai out of season is full of Brits, brutish, burnt to a crisp and tattooed to the gills. Living in Knightsbridge and commuting between Jermyn Street and Berkeley Square, I hadn't realized all these years just how ghastly my adoptive countrymen really are. It was like being in Pentonville again, except for the guards being Greek this time. So I got back on my boat and told the captain to head back slowly to Piraeus, with yet again the girl-gathering operation being as successful as that mounted by Jimmy Carter against the Ayatollah in 1978.

Needless to say, it hasn't been all one big defeat. Last week I also flew to Zante, my father's birthplace, to visit a hotel we own, and boost the morale of the workers (a bit like Mountbatten visiting the sailors in hospital after he managed to get them blown out of the water while looking for glory).

I say it hasn't been one long defeat because I made it safe and sound to Zante while flying Olympic Airways. While the doors were still open and sweaty types were pouring in, the old lady next to me asked me if we were airborne. After I gave her a quick lesson in aerodynamics (I was a Ph.D. at MIT) we were finally airborne and no sooner were we than she got up and tried to open the door, thinking it was the lavatory. She was tackled by the steward and I had to explain to him that a lady who thinks a plane is flying when the doors are still open obviously cannot be held responsible for wanting to step outside for a little pee.

But it got better once on the ground back in Athens. When a woman was told she could not board the plane because she was carrying a live chicken, she actually killed the poor animal right there and then and said, 'OK, no more live chicken, only pistachios and vegetables.' She was allowed to get on.

· Gang show ·

In the years of my youth, a period as it now seems approximating the Battle of Marathon, I counted among my many British friends such over-achievers as Charles Benson, Sir William Pigott-Brown, Rupert Deen, Dai Llewelyn, Nigel Dempster and Lord Lucan. With the exception of his lordship, what united us all was a love for hookers and drink, Lucky Lucan being addicted to the latter but monogamous by nature, a great failing as it turned out.

Although his disappearance did not affect us *per se*, soon after Lucky dropped out things began to change. Benson got out of debt, fathered a daughter and married a respectable girl, not necessarily in that order. William Pigott-Brown went into business and emerged much the poorer for it. Alas, poor Rupert Deen decided to go to work, a catastrophic decision in retrospect. Dirty Dai also became ... er ... respectable, by fronting nightclubs for people who think Pentonville is a school. Yours truly turned into an intellectual and gave up ladies of the night for young girls who look virginal but could teach the pros a thing or two. Dempster, needless to say, left Lloyd's and became the greatest diarist since Madame La Tour du Pin. In fact, he even began to look like her. The old gang had changed for good. But not really.

Last week, while in the process of distancing myself from rowdy Jeffrey Bernard fans queuing for tickets in Soho, I drove to the furthermost western part of London and ran into my old buddies by chance. Nothing had changed but the size of their waistlines. There were more empty wine bottles on the table than Fergie has new best friends, the talk was about the horrendous lack of good hookers nowadays, and bets were being placed over the telephone with interruptions for imbibing and the occasional bite.

No, the soiled miseries of domesticity had not as yet afflicted this little group, although Dai Llewelyn did try to raise a family and further suffocate an overpopulated world. Ditto Nigel, who has really let the side down by making his marriage work. William and Rupert, of course, have remained the *chevaliers sans peur et sans reproche*. They are still wenching and boozing it up, and I sat at their table envying them not a little bit. And reminiscing quite a lot. About fifteen years ago William had me to stay at his wonderful house in the country and gave me the best room in the place. I was with the mother of my children and after a very liquid dinner she and I went to bed and everyone immediately followed. I was rather touched, because they were treating me like royalty of the pre-Fergie type.

But Alexandra had a bee in her bonnet that night and she accused me of something that led to a fight, and we turned our backs on each other, read the newspapers and went to sleep. In the morning Charles Benson was the first to boo, followed by the host and the rest of the motley crew. It seems everyone had gone to bed early in order to watch the show through a strategically placed two-way mirror, but our little tiff had spoiled it. So much so that poor William had to apologize to his guests. Needless to say, I haven't been asked since.

On the day we all lunched together we discovered that it was the anniversary of Dai Llewelyn's getting engaged to three girls simultaneously thirteen years before. So more drinks were called for, more bets were placed, and then it was time for some serious searching for ladies. That is when I left my old gang to their old tricks and went home as a man my age should. And if you believe that you'll believe anything.

· That sinking feeling ·

Palm Beach · Living in Palm Beach is like making love to a beautiful woman who insists on reading a gossip column during the exercise. Better yet, it is like living with a woman whose exquisite looks have been designed by a plastic surgeon. One gets tired of them rather quickly. When I was young and didn't know any better I took the place seriously, but wisdom has finally opened my eyes. The place is a Gulag for the rich, the last refuge of the lifted, a Mecca for the monosyllabic. The nicest thing I can say for its denizens is that they suffer from halitosis of the intellect.

To make matters worse, it rained for the four days I was down there, which meant my children and their tutor spent their time indoors ordering goodies at a clip which would make Jackie Onassis green with envy. In fact, no one since D-Day has prayed more fervently for sunshine than the poor, little Greek boy, but it was not to be. The first ray that hit me was when I wearily climbed inside a TWA hearse for the flight back to the Bagel, and even that one was short-lived. The ghastly woman next to me asked me to pull down the blind as the rays were bouncing off her diamond and blinding her.

Needless to say, there are some nice people in Palm Beach, but as the great Marx (Groucho) once said, not this time. Mind you, it could have been worse. I could have rented a house on the beach and had a large and greasy tanker park itself in my swimming pool. This actually happened back in 1984, during the Thanksgiving holiday, to a friend of mine, Mollie Wilmot, of trademark sunglasses and flowing blonde mane. Mollie, who is brassier than a Sousa band, was sitting down to dinner and about to give thanks for her Picassos and Miros when her maid came in and announced that more guests had arrived on their yacht.

Mollie was perplexed, but only for a moment. When she went out on her patio to welcome the late arrivals she heard only Spanish. She thought it was Reinaldo Herrera, or perhaps someone less chic, say Oscar de la Renta, but what she got was a 193-foot tanker that had broken free of its moorings and had docked right into her swimming pool. The crew was Venezuelan and rather frightened, so Mollie brought them inside for dinner. The captain, needless to mention, had disappeared, as did some of her guests when they realized they were not getting Herrera.

The boat's name was *Mercedes*, and she stayed in Mollie's pool for three months, until she was finally salvaged on 5 March 1985. Mollie threw a goodbye party for her and the skeleton crew, but on 30 March the *Mercedes* was sunk off Fort Lauderdale as an artificial reef. It seems her owners could not afford the salvage, and the port of Palm Beach wouldn't have her, so down she went. Mollie insisted *Mercedes* was sunk because after three months among the Palm Beach crowd she had become unstable and was suffering from severe depression. Being a sailor, I agree. Ships are like people, but they have more feelings. Three months in Palm Beach will kill anyone, especially a sensitive soul like a 193-foot tanker. This is why I only stayed four days and need to go on a holiday next week to get over them.

1990

· All about Eves ·

New York · Leave it to a woman. In the year the Berlin Wall came crumbling down, the mother of my children erected her own by stipulating that no bimbo, not even a nubile young thing or two, would be allowed across the threshold for our annual Christmas Eve party. The result, needless to say, was that my bash turned out to be a rather tame affair, almost as depressing as I imagine one of those ghastly Harold Pinter 'I hate Maggie' soirées must be like.

Mind you, the seating arrangements were OK. As always, I sat between the best looking mother and daughter combo in the world – Carolina Herrera senior and junior – a fact that helped alleviate the boredom of sudden respectability. What was less interesting was the policy of exclusion as practised by my guru, Professor van den Haag, and young Carolina against yours truly. My guru is well into his seventies and Carolina nearing her nineteenth year, but between them no one managed to get the proverbial word in edgewise. Carolina is studying bio-psychology at Vassar, a relatively new subject that the good professor once taught along with law. At the end of the four-hour dialogue the truly beautiful Carolina announced that the prof was cool, and promptly went home. After that it was all downhill.

One week later, however, the trend was reversed, and reversed with a vengeance. As I don't think I've ever met anyone except for myself who actually likes New Year's Eve, I decided to do something about it. (I love the fact that on New Year's Eve I can do what I do every night – get roaring drunk – but without a guilty conscience). Reinaldo Herrera and myself took over Mortimer's, hired a black jazz band, and invited 100 of our closest and dearest, as well as some nocturnal friends of ours one would never dream of presenting to polite society.

The result was predictable. Although at Eton I was taught never to brag, it was one of the best parties for a long time, in fact the best New Year's one ever. I guess the mix of sweet young things, business, books and nightclub characters is what did it. Name-dropping ain't my style, but what the heck? The Nineties are upon us, so I might as well start them right. From the world of people who can also read the captions to pictures came such heavyweights as Norman Mailer and Carlos Fuentes, Dominick Dunne, Peter Maas, Bob Tyrrell and Lewis (Lou to the liberals who seemed to be everywhere that night) Lapham. The nubile ones got excited when a certain Mr Matt Dillon arrived, a young man who my little girl tells me is a film star, but one whom I knew only as a polite soul I spent an evening psychobabbling with at a downtown place called Peggy Sue's. There was Chuck Pfeiffer, my old Vietnam hero buddy who has disgraced himself by appearing in the most anti-American film ever – something about being born on the 4 July – and Roffredo Gaetani, the once noble Roman and ex-pro boxer who at present has turned into a sex object for Big Bagel ladies. There was Philip Niarchos and Edward (Zaharoff) Ullmann, and others much too poor to mention. Oh yes, I almost forgot. Behind the jazz band lay Anthony Haden-Guest, who welcomed the Nineties in the same manner he has welcomed the last three decades, out cold.

Needless to say, I missed Adnan Khashoggi's party due to drink, as well as Philip Niarchos's, which began immediately after mine. But it didn't matter. The year's end celebrations had started early for me this time. They began in London last week on my way to the Bagel. That is when I met the divine Miss Katie Braine, once erroneously described in the world's greatest magazine as a rubber sculptress. (She sculpts in bronze and marble.) They continued at Fellini's, the best London nightspot at the moment, in the company of Bill Lovelady, and went on far into the night at Claridge's, where I now have to bunk, as my flat burned down in my absence. Well, it could have been worse. I could have been at Oscar de la Renta's with Henry Kravis and the rest of the gang.

· Index ·

Index